INTRODUCTION	
BEACH MAP	5
BEACHES with LIFEGUARDS	6
PUBLIC TRANSPORT	6
KEY GUIDE	6
BEACH GUIDE	7
BIBLIOGRAPHY	124

Disclaimer

Although the author has visited every beach in an effort to ensure that the information in this book was accurate at the time of publication, the effects of the weather and the sea can change the topography of the coast and beaches, and alter the accessibility of beaches. Therefore, the author does not assume and hereby disclaims any liability to any party for any loss, damage, or disruption caused by errors or omissions, whether such errors or omissions result from negligence, accident, or any other cause.

INTRODUCTION

The fourth in the *50 Beaches of Cornwall* series visits the north coast and features some of the finest beaches in Cornwall and the whole of the UK. The book is centred around the two popular, but very different holiday towns of Padstow and Newquay. Padstow shelters deep inside the sand-strewn Camel Estuary and we visit beaches on both sides of the river, including those close to the trendy villages of Rock and Polzeath. After leaving the estuary we travel along the stark, rugged, and frequently windswept Atlantic coast where the cliffs are pounded by the restless sea; even on windless days the Atlantic swell comes rolling in, a feature which helps to make this coast the centre of British surfing. It's a coastline of sheer cliffs, protruding headlands, grotesquely-shaped stacks and tenebrous caves; there's a succession of fabulous beaches, with huge inlets, sweeping bays and vast expanses of sand, including the massive Watergate Bay and the spectacular Bedruthan Steps. The town of Newquay may not appeal to everyone but no-one can deny the beauty of its beaches, although it may be preferable to avoid the crowds by visiting outside the main summer season. Even after Newquay the fabulous beaches continue with Crantock and Holywell Bay, one of the undoubted stars of the BBC's Poldark series, and many of the beaches are westerly or north-westerly facing, making them perfect for glorious sunsets. Perranporth, Chapel Porth and Porthtowan follow, and finally there is Portreath with its tiny embattled harbour, and beyond it the North Cliffs, where a number of small beaches lie at the bottom of precipitous paths, with access made even more dangerous by the friable nature of the cliffs. Because of this these beaches have been listed together under the name 'North Cliff Beaches', with emphasis given to the one with slightly easier access, Fishing Cove. Coastal erosion is a problem all along the coast, resulting in several beaches being omitted, notably Big Guns Cove (SW872 760), Pepper Cove (SW855 736), Fox Cove (SW855 732), and Beacon Cove (SW844 666). The last two mentioned are particularly beautiful and the author has spent many happy hours on them, but erosion has resulted in access that is far too dangerous to be recommended. Despite their absence there are more than enough glorious beaches in this book to satisfy even the most pernickety curmudgeon.

There has been a longstanding marketing campaign, *7 Bays for 7 Days*, featuring some of the beaches near Padstow; the question is, why stop at seven days? There's seven weeks worth of fantastic beaches along this stretch of coast, and almost all of them could lay claim to being somebody's favourite. I hope that this guide will help the reader in their joyous quest to find their own beach paradise.

BEACH MAP

1 Pentireglaze	**2** Polzeath
3 Greenaway	**4** Daymer Bay
5 Brea Beach	**6** Rock
7 Porthilly Cove	**8** Oldtown Cove
9 Dennis Cove	**10** Padstow Town Bar
11 Chidley Pumps	**12** St George's Cove
13 Tregirls Beach	**14** Hawker's Cove
15 Trevone	**16** Newtrain Bay
17 Harlyn Bay	**18** Onjohn –Boat Cove
19 Onjohn – Cellars	**20** Mother Ivey's
21 Booby's Bay	**22** Constantine
23 Treyarnon Bay	**24** Porthcothan
25 Porth Mear	**26** Pentire Steps
27 Bedruthan Steps	**28** Mawgan Porth
29 Watergate Bay	**30** Whipsiderry
31 Porth	**32** Lusty Glaze
33 Tolcarne	**34** Great Western
35 Towan	**36** Newquay Harbour
37 Little Fistral	**38** Fistral Beach
39 River Gannel	**40** Crantock
41 Porth Joke	**42** Holywell Bay
43 Penhale Sands	**44** Perranporth
45 Trevellas Porth	**46** Trevaunance Cove
47 Chapel Porth	**48** Porthtowan
49 Portreath	**50** North Cliff Beaches

BEACHES with LIFEGUARDS

A. Easter - end October: Fistral Beach (north).

B. Early May- end September, October weekends and half term: Polzeath, Haryln Bay, Constantine Bay, Mawgan Porth, Watergate Bay, Towan Beach, Perranporth, Porthtowan.

C. Early May - end September: Treyarnon Bay

D. Mid-May - end September: Trevone, Booby's Bay, Porthcothan, Porth, Tolcarne, Great Western, Crantock, Holywell Bay, Penhale Sands, Trevaunance Cove, Chapel Porth, Portreath.

E. Early July - end August: Lusty Glaze, Fistral Beach (south), Crantock (river end).

PUBLIC TRANSPORT

First Kernow

47 Truro - Camborne - for Portreath
85 Newquay - Truro for Crantock, Holywell Bay
87 Newquay - Truro for Crantock, Holywell Bay, Perran Sands, Perranporth, St Agnes
96 Wadebridge - Bude for Rock, Polzeath
A4 Newquay - St Ives for Perran Sands, Perranporth, St Agnes, Porthtowan, Portreath, Hell's Mouth (2 a day)
A5 - Newquay - Padstow for Porth, Watergate Bay, Mawgan Porth, Bedruthan Steps, Porthcothan, Constantine (village) Harlyn Bay, Trevone Turn
11A Bodmin Parkway - Padstow - Plymouth Citybus

Hopleys Coaches

304 Porthtowan – Truro
315 St Agnes – Redruth

Summercourt Travel

408 Newquay – Airport for Porth, Mawgan Porth

KEY GUIDE

P	Parking
PT	Public Transport
RP	Rock Pools
SF	Surfing
SW	Swimming
L	Lifeguards
DA	Dogs Allowed
DR	Dogs Restricted

1. PENTIREGLAZE HAVEN
SW 935 796
P, PT, RP, SW, DR

Our journey along the coast begins on the east side of Padstow Bay at Pentireglaze Haven and its tiny neighbour, Pentire Haven, which shelter in the lee of Pentire Point, just to the north of the perpetually popular Polzeath. Known locally as Baby Bay, a visit to Pentireglaze at high water reveals a pleasant, westerly-facing cove around 80yds wide with a beach perhaps 45yds deep, but as the tide recedes it stretches to more than 250yds to join up with the beach at Polzeath. A small stream runs down the middle of the fine, golden sand and the flanks are lined with rock outcrops; there used to be a couple of notable caves, Breakneck Cavern and Billy's Cavern, but the former collapsed in 2018. Slipper Point, which separates the beach from Polzeath at low water, is a good place to examine Polzeath Slate with its distinctive purple and green coloured rocks, formed around 400 million years ago. Pentireglaze derives from the Cornish *pen*, 'head', *tir*, 'land', and *glas,* 'green or blue'.

Due to its proximity to Polzeath the beach can be busy during the summer season, but when the wind blows it has a raw, untamed atmosphere that was put to good use in 1892 when Sabine Baring-Gould set his novel *In the Roar of the Sea* here, based on the tales of a semi-legendary smuggler, Cruel Coppinger. He described the cove as a 'harbour and den of every lawless character along the coast', a place of 'wild uproar' and 'reckless revelry', traits that were apparent when shipwreck scenes for the 1983 version of *Jamaica Inn* were filmed here, featuring

Jane Seymour as a very glamorous Mary Yellan. Those wrecks were fictitious, but in 1843 a brig, *Hope*, from Fishguard and laden with copper ore, attempted to ride out a storm in the sheltered estuary but was driven onto the rocks here, resulting in the deaths of all seven of the crew.

Pentire Haven is a narrow inlet to the north of Pentireglaze. South facing, it's completely covered at high water but as the tide ebbs a delightful mixture of shingle, sand, pebbles and rock platforms is revealed. A small stream runs down the beach, but the unbroken flat sand only emerges at low water when it links with the whole bay. Swimming is not recommended here and it's only possible at Pentireglaze on a rising high tide, making sure to stay well within the cove itself. Safety equipment can be found by the access path to Pentireglaze. The lifeguards who patrol Polzeath cover both beaches when the tide is out but not when they are cut off from the rest of the bay, and it's much safer to swim in the designated safe area at Polzeath. There may be a few rock pools to explore at low water, while dog restrictions apply throughout the summer. There's easy access to both beaches from the Coast Path. The nearest car park is in New Polzeath, with a little roadside parking available on Atlantic Terrace, although finding a space during the summer is tricky, and Gulland Road, which is also where the public toilets are situated. There's also a small car park close to Pentire Farm, followed by a walk of around ¾ of a mile. That car park is on the site of a silver and lead mine which peaked between 1850 and 1875 when it produced 955 tons of lead ore and 19,065 ounces of silver. The mine's engine house was demolished in 1957. Mining took place in this area for around 400 years but human activity has been around for much longer, as evidenced by a Bronze Age burial barrow, which was dug out sometime in the past, on the cliffs above the beach. On the northeast side of Pentire Head is a distinctive promontory called The Rumps, site of an Iron Age cliff castle, and a walk around the headland is highly recommended, not just for the panoramic views but also because Laurence Binyon reputedly wrote his most moving poem, *For the Fallen,* while sitting on the cliffs in 1914, commemorated by a stone plaque erected in 2001. The headland is also a good place to spot dolphins on their way in or out of the Camel Estuary. The amazing beach at Polzeath attracts thousands of visitors every year, but these fine coves, very different from Polzeath, are far too good to be regarded as mere adjuncts to their famous neighbour and are well worth visiting in their own right.

2. POLZEATH
SW 936 790
P, PT, RP, SF, SW, L, DR

Tucked just inside the Camel Estuary, Polzeath is regarded as one of the best all-round beaches in Cornwall, with plenty to delight families, surfers, and devotees of wild, unspoilt beaches. Its only fault is that it gets incredibly busy during the summer season, so a visit at other times of the year, when it's still beautiful, may be advisable.

At high water the beach is over 200yds wide and 150yds deep, although there will be less sand during spring tides and in the winter. In summer, though, this area is invariably packed and it's only as the tide recedes that the magic occurs, with the sea retreating for up to 600 yards at low water, revealing an almost flat beach of fine golden sand with perhaps an occasional patch of shingle. A stream splits the back of the beach in two, only fanning out after passing the high water mark. Approaching the sea, the beach opens up gloriously to link with Pentireglaze and Pentire Haven to the north and extending to tiny Trestram Cove in the south, a distance of some 800yds. Cartographers refer to this expanse of sand as Hayle Bay, from the Cornish *heyl,* 'estuary', but the name isn't commonly used. Trestram is usually the quietest part of the beach and is sheltered from the prevailing westerly winds; it is, though, quickly cut off from the main beach as the tide rises. Another sheltered area, at least from northerly winds, is Cockett Haven, which lies below New Polzeath; very popular, it's also cut off by the incoming tide but has its own access path.

On both sides of the beach there are rocky areas containing easily discernable purple and greyish-green bands of Polzeath slate, and there are usually plenty of rock pools, especially on the southern side. The beach and the rocky areas that surround it are part of a Voluntary Marine Conservation Area containing 10 species of seaweed and several species of shellfish, crustaceans and molluscs that are recognised as being of special conservation importance, including the tiny Celtic sea slug and rare red Polysiphonia seaweeds.

Polzeath is the first of the major surfing beaches that we'll encounter on this trip along the north coast. Westerly facing and right at the mouth of the Camel Estuary, it receives the full force of the Atlantic swell, while the gently shelving beach produces long and slow breaking waves that make ideal conditions for all levels of surfing, from beginner to expert; it's also ideal for paddling on calm days.

There are regular surfing competitions and three surf schools operate close to the beach, *George's Surf School, Surf's Up,* and *Wavehunters*. In the summer it's important to keep to the designated surfing area, which is often crowded when conditions are favourable. It's not ideal for swimming because of dangerous currents, especially at low water; it may be possible, with care, in very calm conditions at high water, but it's best to wait until the RNLI Lifeguards are present, keeping to the areas they designate as safe. It's not usually suitable for snorkelling but in calm conditions at high water it can be worthwhile, especially around Slipper Point and Trestram Cove. There are a number of safety equipment points above the beach.

Parking isn't easy during the summer despite two large car parks, with the main one big enough for around 900 cars; it also provides splendid views of the beach. The second car park is in New Polzeath, while there is also a little roadside parking allowed on Atlantic Terrace; these are best for Cockett Haven, with steps leading directly to the beach. Additional parking is allowed on the back of the beach itself, whenever tides permit; whether that is a good idea probably depends on whether you have a car or not! Access from there and the main car park is easy. Dog restrictions apply throughout the summer. In the beach car parking area the *Beach Box Café* invariably does a roaring trade and there are plenty of other cafés and restaurants offering a wide range of food and drink, some with balconies and terraces to take advantage of the amazing views. There are a couple of general stores and several gift shops. Various children's activities are available on Coronation Gardens, just across the road from the beach, and nestled on the lane between there and the shops is *Polzeath Marine Centre,* with information boards, games, activities and leaflets. The public toilets are near there, too, with more on Gulland Road in New Polzeath

The name comes from the Cornish *pol,* 'cove' and *sygh,* 'dry', presumably because of the vast beach at low water. The village is split into two, Old and New, but there is little of the charm found in most Cornish coastal villages: even the 'old' part is mainly a 20th century development dedicated to the burgeoning tourist industry. New Polzeath has a handful of seafront Edwardian houses and a few inter-war bungalows, but is mainly a post-WW2 development which gained its name in 1972; previously it was called Pentireglaze. What history there is mainly concerns the beach: in 1796 a 65ft whale carcass was washed ashore, its odorous body cut up and carried away to be used as manure by local farmers. On 29th December 1865 the barque *Juliet,* bound for London with a cargo of Demerara rum and sugar, was wrecked in the estuary with much of the cargo washing up on the beach and its surrounds. All 17 of the crew were rescued by the Padstow lifeboat and 280 casks of rum salvaged, while any overproof rum, mixed with seawater, was eagerly scooped out of hollows in the rocks. Scenes for the 1950 David Lean film, *Madeleine*, were shot here, with the star, Ann Todd, required to ride a bolting horse across the beach and into the sea where she was to be rescued by her lover. Unfortunately, the horse really did bolt, causing the terrified star to cling grimly to the saddle; she refused to remount for a re-shoot, necessary because holidaymakers could be seen in the background, so her understudy heroically took to the saddle instead. More recently the beach has been graced by royalty (Princes William and Harry), politicians (David Cameron) and a whole host of celebrities, major and minor.

Both parts of the village enjoy fabulous views of the bay with its magnificent stretch of golden sand and the green cliffs of Pentire Head. A deceptive 1½ miles offshore from the beach is Newland, a 165ft high island that is home to seabirds such as cormorants, shags, and even the occasional puffin, and provides a restful haven for grey seals.

The crowds that flock to Polzeath during the summer will be off-putting for some and to see the beach at its best it's definitely advisable to visit outside the peak season; if that is not possible then seek out the more secluded nooks. There are also superb walks available to the quieter beaches in the area, featuring stunning views from the Coast Path.

3. GREENAWAY BEACH and BROADAGOGUE COVE
SW 928 783 and SW 929 785
RP, SW, DA

Anyone seeking to escape the summer scrum at Polzeath would be well advised to seek out these very different and little known beaches, just a short walk away at Trebetherick. Greenaway is the name given to the unspoilt cliffs between Polzeath and Daymer Bay, and both it and Trebetherick have been immortalised in the work of the former Poet Laureate, Sir John Betjeman, who enjoyed childhood holidays here and later bought a house in the village. He is buried in the nearby St Enodoc churchyard. From the main car park on the cliffs above Polzeath it's a walk of around 800yds to the first path and steps down to Greenaway Beach – there's no direct access to Broadagogue. Alternatively, parking at Daymer Bay allows a shorter walk around Trebetherick Point to the first of several paths down to the beach.

Broadagogue is completely covered at high water but a thin strip of sand and shingle usually survives at Greenaway; this expands to over 250yds in length at low water. The ebbing tide soon unveils the main feature of both beaches as a low rocky reef appears, bearing the distinctive purple and green bands associated with Polzeath Slate, and by low water it's possible to scramble over the rocks to Broadagogue, which also features a large patch of sand at low water and there's a secret cave to look out for, but it's vital to keep an eye on the incoming sea and check the tide times before visiting. Beyond the sand, Greenaway continues southwards for over 300yds to Trebetherick Point, consisting mainly of

12

rock platforms and outcrops, with plenty of rock pools. Dogs are allowed on both beaches.

Swimming is not recommended at low water because of submerged rocks and offshore currents, but it is possible with care on a rising high tide on calm days. There is no safety equipment. It's not really a surfing beach but low water may attract a few experienced surfers in the right conditions; it's not suitable for the inexperienced. There is a café and shop at Daymer Bay and shops, restaurants and pubs at Polzeath, with public toilets at both.

There have been numerous wrecks at Greenaway as ships attempted to reach the shelter of Padstow in stormy weather, and wreckage can be seen amongst the rocks at the southern end. One of the most tragic occurred on 11th April 1900 when the ketch *Peace and Plenty* struck Greenway Rocks in a fierce storm. The Padstow lifeboat, *Arab,* was launched and anchored close to the stricken ship, but a huge wave struck the lifeboat, breaking ten oars and washing eight of her crew overboard. The men managed to scramble back onboard without loss of life but, due to the lack of oars, the boat was incapacitated. Using the remaining oars and the anchor cable, the coxswain skilfully manoeuvred the boat into a creek where the crew jumped ashore, moments before she was dashed against the rocks. The steam lifeboat, *James Stevens no.4,* was launched, but on leaving the harbour it was caught by a heavy swell and capsized; eight of her crew of eleven were drowned. The Trebetherick rocket brigade managed to attach lines to the *Peace and Plenty* just before it sank beneath the surface, saving the lives of five of the eight man crew. Wrecks can still occur even in modern times: on the morning of 5th September 2017, a stricken fishing trawler, the Cornish registered *Le Men Du,* ran aground but was re-floated on the evening high tide.

Greenaway and Broadagogue may not have the huge sandy shores of their neighbours but they are ideally placed between two popular beaches as a perfect spot for rock pool fans, shell-seekers, geologists and those keen to escape the crowds. While Broadagogue is delightful, any visit needs to be carefully planned, but Greenaway is completely unspoilt and provides a perfect picnic spot for those enjoying a walk along the springy, turf covered cliffs between Polzeath and Daymer Bay. Definitely worth a visit!

4. DAYMER BAY
SW 928 776
P, PT, RP, SW, DA

Set in the heart of 'Betjeman country', Daymer Bay is a gloriously sandy beach, surrounded by idyllic countryside and with fabulous views across the estuary to Stepper Point. The westerly facing beach is backed by a small dune system, protected by a fence, and bounded by Trebetherick Point to the north and the distinctive hump of Brea Hill to the south. At high water there's a lengthy, but thin, strip of sand but at low water the tide retreats for over 475yds, leaving a vast expanse of flat golden sand that, when it merges with Brea Beach, forms a glorious and very popular walk all the way to Rock. Towards Trebetherick Point there's a scattering of low rock outcrops, the only area likely to contain rock pools. A small stream runs from the corner of the beach, dispersing shortly after the high water mark. Across the estuary, the sandy Harbour Cove looks temptingly close, but the estuary channel should never be entered due to powerful currents. Swimming in the bay is possible on a rising high tide, and there's some good snorkelling around Trebetherick Point. At high water it's possible to wade out for quite a way before the water reaches waist height. Conditions can occasionally be favourable for surfing, but wind surfing, SUP, and kite surfing are more popular, although the latter is restricted during July and August. There is safety equipment above the beach. Dogs are allowed all year.

The remains of a 4,400 year old forest can sometimes be seen at low spring tides, while Neolithic shell mounds and fossil soils containing snails, some now rare or extinct in Cornwall, are often exposed after winter storms.

During WW2 the bay was protected from invasion by a high metal screen built across the beach; barbed wire entanglements were placed in front and the

14

dunes planted with mines. Thankfully the defences were never needed but there were casualties: several inquisitive dogs were blown up and one RAF man, home on leave, was dared by his sisters to cross the minefield, with fatal consequences.

Beyond the dunes, quirkily situated in the middle of a golf course, is the delightful St Enodoc Church where John Betjeman was buried after his death in 1984. Located amid sand dunes, it was constantly threatened with inundation, and by the 16th century the sand was such a problem that the church was known as 'Sinking Neddy'. By the 18th century it had become completely submerged in the sand, but it was necessary to hold at least one service annually to maintain the tithes, so each year the intrepid vicar and parishioners were lowered into the sanctuary through a hole in the roof. It was not until 1863 that the church was rescued from its sandy grave to be cleaned and restored, while the dunes were stabilised to prevent further inundation. The church is believed to be built on the site of a cave where Enodoc dwelt as a hermit in the 6th century following his or her arrival from Wales; it's unclear whether Enodoc was male or female. St Petroc also landed here in the 6th century. There is a path from Daymer Bay to the church, but care needs to be taken when crossing the golf course where it's important to keep to the marked path. St Enodoc's and the beach feature prominently in Justin Cartwright's 2004 novel, *The Promise of Happiness*.

Although off the beaten track compared to its neighbours, Rock and Polzeath, Daymer Bay can be very busy in the summer, mainly because it's blessed with its own car park, big enough for 300 cars but often full on sunny days. The car park lies at the end of a long and narrow road, which can be chaotic in the summer; it was once a 'sanding lane', used by farmers when carting away loads of sand to spread on fields as fertiliser. There's easy access to the beach via a small set of steps. The nearest bus stop is around 750yds away by the *Mowhay Café* on Ham Field in Trebetherick. Seasonal toilets are located in the car park, where there is also a café and a well-stocked beach shop.

Probably the best way to reach the beach is to catch the ferry from Padstow to Rock and then walk northwards, either along Brea Beach or the Coast Path. It's well over a mile but definitely worth the effort, and on a quiet day with an ebbing tide, as the turquoise water laps gently against the shore, it's possible to emulate the young Betjeman and be "the monarch of miles of sand."

5. BREA BEACH
SW 927 759
P, SW, DA

Beautiful Brea Beach is cut off from Daymer Bay at high water by the grassy tump of Bray Hill, and at that stage of the tide it consists of a thin strip of sand backed by a marram-clad sand dune system. As the tide ebbs a long stretch of golden sand is revealed, extending for over 900yds to Cassock Hill, where it merges with Rock Beach, and by low water it's possible to stroll along the deliciously soft sand all the way from Rock to Daymer Bay, a very popular route for dog walkers as their pets are allowed on all three beaches. The sand dunes protrude into the centre of the beach with a triangular spit of sand beneath them; the spit has been building in recent years and be aware that at its extremities the sand is exceptionally soft and capable of trapping a person. There are also abnormally strong tidal currents in the shallow water over this sand, and it is more than capable of taking a person off their feet; it's therefore important to be extremely cautious if venturing into this area.

Swimming is only possible on a rising high tide and should definitely not be attempted in the channel at low water because of very strong currents and steeply shelving sand. Windsurfing is a popular activity when the winds and tides are suitable. There is no safety equipment and it's not a beach for rock pools. All facilities can be found in Rock, and the nearest parking is the Quarry Car Park; at low water it's an easy walk along the sand from Rock but at high water there's a walk of over 400yds to reach the beach, with easy access from the dunes. It's also

16

possible to park at Daymer Bay, followed by a longer walk around Bray Hill. Bus users are advised to disembark at Trebetherick, by the *Mowhay Café* on Ham Field, with a lengthy walk to follow, either via Daymer Bay or St Enodoc Church.

'Brea' and 'bray' are interchangeable, but Betjeman favoured the latter when referring to the hill, perhaps because of the more obvious pronunciation, or maybe because *brea* or *bre* translates as 'hill'. The steep climb to the 203ft summit is well worth the effort for the spectacular views of the estuary and the surrounding countryside, including a birds-eye view of St Enodoc Church eccentrically interned in a hollow in the middle of a golf course. There are also a number of easily discernable Bronze Age burial mounds on the summit.

The sand dune system behind the beach provides a wonderful setting for *St Enodoc Golf Club*, which was established in 1890 and immortalised in Betjeman's poem, *Seaside Golf*. An 18 hole course was laid out in 1907 and altered in the 1920s; known as the 'Church Course', it's notable for the cavernous 'Himalaya' bunker on its 6th hole. A second, slightly less demanding course, the 'Holywell Course', was completed in 1982. The name is inspired by the well used by Enodoc to baptise his converts, situated close to the 12th hole.

Because the two are linked, many people mistakenly regard Brea as part of Rock Beach, but the sand dunes and the hill help to create a more tranquil atmosphere and, certainly towards the hill, it tends to be much quieter than either of its neighbours.

6. ROCK
SW 929 756
P, PT, DA

'Chelsea-on-Sea', 'Kensington of Cornwall', and 'Britain's St Tropez' are just three of the nicknames bestowed upon the former riverside hamlet of Rock, due to its popularity with highly affluent visitors. The village has the highest proportion of second homes in Cornwall, with many rich, famous and, in some cases, powerful individuals owning property in the area. Development began as far back as the 1930s, and by the 1950s there were already signs of over development, with a plethora of planning applications passed with undue haste. By the 1970s Rock was fast becoming an area of second or holiday homes with land values rocketing and properties priced well beyond the reach of local residents, a process that has continued through to the present day with houses selling for mind-boggling prices. The result is a somewhat sprawling village with no distinct centre; its shops are scattered and there's no church, but the majority of restaurants and cafés are by the waterfront. All this is a far cry from the tiny hamlet that existed here in the 14th century when it was part of the Manor of *Penmayn*, 'head of stones'. By 1337 the hamlet was known as *Blaketore*, which was anglicised in the 18th century to Black Rock, later shortened to Rock. The rock referred to was, until the late 19th century, visible close to the present northern ferry landing site, and is memorialized in the name of the ferry that links Rock to Padstow, the *Black Tor Ferry*. A ferry has operated here since 1337.

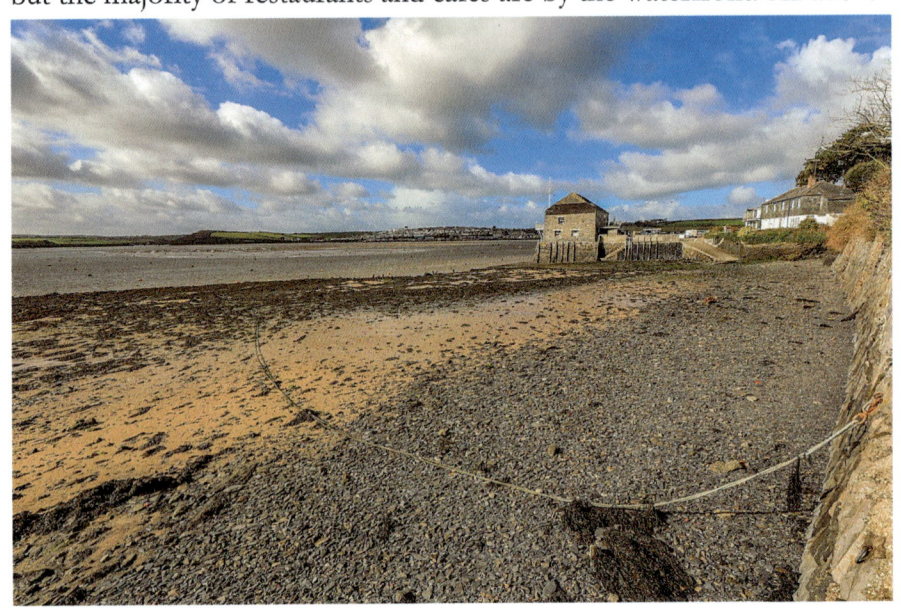

Throughout the summer the sheltered waters off Rock Beach are popular for sailing, canoeing, dinghy racing, windsurfing, waterskiing and angling, and the sand is often littered with numerous dinghies and other small craft. There are thriving sailing and ski schools, and boats for various activities can be hired. With the increase in water-based activities the RNLI have stationed a 'D' Class lifeboat on the beach to provide cover in case of emergencies.

The most prominent feature of the beach is the old quay and former grain warehouse, once scheduled for demolition but saved and refurbished in 1976; it's now home to the sailing club. The area of beach around the quay, and as far as the ferry slipway, is south facing and at low water consists of mainly sand and shingle, with the rippling sands of the Town Bar stretching towards Padstow. At high water this part of the beach is virtually covered. Beyond the slipway the beach becomes westerly facing with a fair-sized strip of sand above the high water mark and a glorious beach of golden sand at low, when, beneath Cassock Hill, it merges with Brea Beach. It's not famed for rock pools but dogs are allowed all year.

The sheer amount of boating activity makes it unsuitable for swimming. In addition, strong tidal currents make it unsafe at low water, and while it may be possible with care on a rising high tide, it's not recommended to swim amongst the numerous moorings and craft, and with the main estuary channel running close to shore, speeding boats are an additional hazard. There are over 200 moorings for the many types of boating activities, and they can be rented by the day or week. There are several safety equipment points above the beach.

There's easy access to various points of the beach via five slipways, and a car park can be found at the end of the road above the beach on the site of an old quarry - the rock was quarried for use as ballast by sailing ships after unloading their cargoes in Padstow. Public toilets can be found in the car park. The nearest bus stop is over half a mile away by Clock Garage, but the most thrilling way to arrive is definitely by the *Black Tor Ferry* from Padstow.

7. PORTHILLY COVE
SW 936 754
P, PT, SW, DA

The final beach on the eastern side of the Camel is the lovely Porthilly Cove, often incorrectly described as being part of Rock Beach but actually very different in character and atmosphere. It's very much an estuary beach, with wonderful views across to Padstow and Dennis Hill. When the tide is out, the empty salt marsh is bleakly beautiful, with vast sandbanks making it a haven for wading birds, and when the tide is in the river is filled with boats and birds bobbing contentedly on the sparkling water. Fishing has always had an important role in the local economy and it continues today: keep an eye out for specialised crab and shrimp boats, which have lifting keels and shallow draughts to cope with the shallow water. Also operating from the beach are *Rock Shellfish*, who are growers, wholesalers and purifiers of mussels, oysters and clams. They import Pacific oysters as tiny juveniles, and then grow them in cages held on frames on the seabed, which allows them to feed on natural plankton and flourish in the clean waters of the estuary. Mussels are also bought in as juveniles and laid on mussel beds in the estuary.

Sheltered, and always much quieter than Rock, low water reveals a beach of flat, firm sand, some 300yds deep and 265yds wide, dissected by a small stream, with patches of shingle and low outcrops, especially on the southern side. Beyond the beach are lengthy sandbanks and mud flats, a favourite spot for fishermen digging for lugworms, and a walk over to Padstow looks deceptively feasible, but it should certainly never be attempted. It is possible, though, to walk over an area of shingle and low outcrops to Rock, but at high water the two beaches are disconnected, Porthilly reduced to just a narrow strip of sand, shingle and small stones. It's not a beach for rock pools but dogs are allowed all year. Swimming is only possible at high water, although it tends to be very shallow, and it's not advisable to swim outside the cove at any stage of the tide. There is no safety equipment.

Adding to the tranquillity of Porthilly is St Michael's Church, nestling just above the shore on the southern bank of the cove. When St Samson landed in the estuary in the 5th century it's likely he came ashore here, but nothing is known of a church building before the present one of 11th and 12th century origin, when it was probably a chapel for the monks of Bodmin Priory. The two old farmhouses by the church gate, *Porthilly Eglos* and *Porthilly Greys*, as in Greyfriars, are thought to have been the House of Labour and House of Rest for the monastic community. The church was substantially restored in 1867, while just outside the main door is a low, medieval four-holed wheel-head cross. A sea wall, lapped by surging tides, protects the grassy churchyard where there are handy seats for taking in the view and waiting for the tide to go out. Stone steps provide easy access to and from the beach and, with an atmosphere of peace and sanctity, the church is well worth a visit.

From Rock Road the beach is approached down the steep and narrow Porthilly Lane, and after around 400yds there is a gated footpath down to the cove. There is a limited amount of roadside parking, but it's important to avoid obstructing the lane and gates. Alternatively, park in Rock and just across from *The Mariners* restaurant and pub there is a short footpath which leads down to the northerly part of the beach. It's a walk of just over half a mile from the nearest bus stop (Clock Garage). All facilities, including public toilets, can be found in Rock.

8. OLDTOWN COVE
SW938 739
P, SW, DA

The closure of the Wadebridge to Padstow railway line on 28th January 1967 led to much wailing and gnashing of teeth, notably by John Betjeman, who had described it as "the most beautiful train journey I know." Years of indecision followed until 1980 when the track was reopened as a footpath and cycle way, *The Camel Trail*, running for 17.3 miles from Wenford Bridge, on Bodmin Moor, to Padstow, with the 5.5 mile section from Wadebridge to Padstow being the most popular part of what is the most cycled off-road trail in the UK. Much of the westerly foreshore of the estuary is accessible from the trail, and roughly 1½ miles south of Padstow is the sheltered and secluded Oldtown Cove.

Consisting mainly of a mixture of grey sand and shingle, it may not have the immediate appeal of the wonderful sandy beaches that we encountered on the eastern side of the river but it's an idyllic spot, beautiful at all stages of the tide: at high water there's just a strip of shingle, while low water unveils patches of yellow estuary sand. Hidden from view by a hawthorn hedge, full of wild flowers in the spring, and accessible by a short, narrow and steep flight of steps, it makes a perfect picnic spot, with views across the estuary to a gently rolling, pastoral landscape. The only disturbance to the tranquillity comes from the occasional ebullient cry of the cyclists speeding obliviously past this underappreciated beauty spot. An arched bridge in the embankment allows the tide to ebb and flow into a creek where Halwyn Manor once stood on the Padstow side, and if the tide is right there will be wading birds feeding, along with herons and little egrets. Across the river, the eye is invariably drawn to the graceful hump of Cant Hill, 250ft high with a name that derives from the Latin *canti*, 'corner', referring to St Minver parish, which juts out into the sea. The county of Kent has the same derivation, while Kent was also a common surname in this area.

It's not a beach for rock pools, but there may be some along the shore on either side of the cove. Swimming is only feasible at high water, but even then strong tidal currents are problematic. There is no safety equipment. Kayaks are sometimes launched from the cove, and it helps that a small car park has been created nearby, at the end of a long and narrow road from St Issey. From the car park, go up the steps and the entrance to the beach can be found 170yds to the left. Dogs are allowed all year.

It's possible that the cove takes its name from an old name for Padstow: in medieval times the town was commonly called *Aldestowe*, 'old place', in contrast to Bodmin, the 'new place', after the monks from St Petroc's monastery fled to Bodmin following a Viking raid in 981. The river name comes from the Cornish *Cam*, 'crooked', and *heyl*, 'estuary'. Oldtown Cove is very much a 'river beach', similar to those found on the Helford or the Fal. A place of gentle charm and stunning scenery, it should definitely be sought out by those seeking a quiet interlude from the more famous beaches nearby.

9. DENNIS COVE
SW 921 744
P, DA

The beach at Dennis Cove has much in common with Oldtown Cove, being a mixture of grey sand, shingle, and small stones, with the distinctive yellow sand of the estuary uncovered at low water. A small strip of shingle and stones survives at high water, but there can often be more mud here than at Oldtown. Dogs are allowed all year. Much of the stony foreshore towards Padstow is accessible, apart from at high water, although it may be necessary to skirt a few muddy incursions, and with free roadside parking available at nearby Porthilly View, this is a popular route for dog walkers. It's not really suitable for swimming; it is possible within the cove at high water, but definitely not on an ebbing tide.

There's no safety equipment, and the beach isn't noted for rock pools, although an occasional one may be discovered along the foreshore. There are fine views across the river, varying from a flat plain of sand, when it's all yellows, blues and greens, to one of shallow water dotted with bobbing boats and yachts. For the best views, however, it's necessary to climb the nearby Dennis Hill, from where there's a panoramic view that encompasses the sea, the whole of the estuary, and, at low water, the glistening acres of sand, with the dunes and hillsides frequently bathed in brilliantly reflected light.

The name comes from the Cornish *dinas*, 'fort', and a hill such as this seems an ideal site for an Iron Age castle, but, surprisingly, no remains have been found. The top of the hill is marked by a 50ft obelisk celebrating Queen Victoria's Jubilee in 1887. The cove was formerly the site of the largest of Padstow's six shipyards, with the first ship being built in 1782. Vessels of up to 800 tons were constructed, while the last ship to be repaired here was *The Teaser*, which, along with sister ships *The Telegraph* and *The Telephone*, was used for carrying slate and stone from Boscastle and Port Gaverne. The ropewalk leading down to the cove was the longest covered one in Cornwall; ropes were produced for shipyards and capstans. Shipbuilding fell into decline in the 1880s as iron ships replaced wooden ones, and this was exacerbated by the arrival of the railway in 1899, which meant fewer ships were needed.

Dennis Cove is far from the best beach on the estuary but it's a pleasant place for a picnic or just to escape the crowds. There are numerous access paths to the stony foreshore, the only hazard being the number of cyclists on the Camel Trail, and there's a slipway to the beach from the Dennis Farm campsite, often used for launching kayaks and dinghies.

10. PADSTOW TOWN BAR BEACH
SW 921 747
P, PT, DA

Padstow shelters in a valley on the west side of the Camel Estuary, which for thousands of years has provided an oasis of calm for ships navigating a safe route along the jagged, unforgiving north coast of Devon and Cornwall. It's been a trading centre for around 4,000 years, while the overland route between Padstow and Fowey linked Ireland with Brittany and was frequently used by monks arriving from Wales and Ireland, some of whom settled locally to spread their message throughout their fellow Celtic nation. A modern version of this ancient link can be followed today, known as *The Saints' Way*, running for roughly 30 miles from Padstow to Fowey and providing an opportunity to explore the beautiful Cornish countryside while appreciating its sacred Celtic heritage. One of the saints who landed in the estuary was Petroc, son of a Welsh prince but educated in Ireland, who built a church in what was to become Padstow. He travelled widely but returned to Cornwall as an old man where he died just outside the town, which soon became a place of pilgrimage and an important ecclesiastical centre; it remained so until it was ransacked by raiding Vikings in 981.

Much of the lower part of Padstow is built on salty alluvial mud, and until around 1700 the tide would have flowed towards the cliff which surrounds the harbour. The first stone pier was built in the 16th century, and the little harbour would have been crammed with vessels exporting slate, metal ores, and fish, with Welsh coal being brought in. In the 19th century it boomed as a fishing port and, when the mining industry collapsed, it became the embarkation port for the thousands of Cornishmen, women and children emigrating to far-flung corners of the world. It's possible to catch a glimpse of this old Padstow in its picturesque harbour, narrow streets and haphazard terraces of houses, but today it's renowned as a tourist favourite and a gourmet's delight, mainly due to the influence of celebrity chef Rick Stein.

Town Bar is the middle of the three sandbars in the Camel Estuary, the others being the infamous Doom Bar near the mouth of the estuary, and Halwyn Bank, found where the estuary changes direction. They are the result of sediment being washed from the sea to collect in the pocket of the Camel, where it stays, clotting into bars of sand across the water. Over 80% of the sediment is derived from marine mollusc shells and as a consequence it has a high calcium content, making it ideal for use as a fertiliser to improve agricultural soil. The sand shifts with every tide, and the estuary is dredged every day to enable access to the port; it's estimated that over 120,000 tons of sand are dredged every year, and an estimated 10 million tons since the early 19th century.

Two fairly steep slipways provide access to the beach, the first a mere 310yds from the harbour car park. High water sees a mixture of shingle, grey sand and patches of mud, but low water unveils the sweeping yellow sands of the bar, the opposite bank of the estuary looking deceptively within reach. Since the early 1970s the beach has been the starting point for an annual one mile charity swim across the estuary, the swimmers leaving from the slipway outside the Sea Cadet building and finishing at the RNLI slipway on Rock Beach. Other than that it's not ideal for swimming due to strong tidal currents, with high water on a calm day the only possibility. There's no safety equipment. Another charity event made its debut in August 2018 when a cricket match was played on the flat sands of the bar, the two innings being rushed through before the tide returned. Played on behalf of the Fisherman's Mission charity, it's hoped that the game will become a fixture in the calendar. Dogs are allowed all year.

A common sight is that of fishermen squelching around on the bar, digging for lugworms. Mussels and razor clams can also be found, and at one time it was a popular site for the harvesting of cockles: it's estimated that over 50 tons were removed each year, with many people earning their sole living from them. Nowadays the cockles are in short supply; locals tend to blame a team of Welsh pickers who descended on the river a few years ago, but the real explanation remains a mystery.

In 2010 the shifting sands of the bar uncovered the remnants of a wreck, thought to be that of the Canadian barque *Antoinette*. She was bound for Santos from Newport, Gwent with a cargo of coal, but drifted onto the Doom Bar in January 1895. All the crew were rescued but part of the wreckage was carried by spring tides onto Town Bar, where it became a hazard to fishermen and ferrymen. An attempt at demolition using gelignite followed, with the resulting explosion so violent that reports suggest every window in the harbour was blown in and the smoke could be seen three miles away! What was left became buried in the sand until it re-emerged, perilously close to a navigational channel. This resulted in another, much smaller attempt to blow it up, and much of the remaining wreck was removed after being recorded by maritime archaeologists.

Padstow has everything the modern visitor requires but retains much of its old Cornish charm, making it a perfect holiday destination. It's surrounded by wonderful beaches, including many better than Town Bar. However, with its rich history, important role in everyday life of the estuary, and the beautiful views it provides, it's a beach that deserves a look.

11. CHIDLEY PUMPS BEACH
SW 922 759
P, PT, SW, DA

The peculiarly named Chidley Pumps Beach is a diminutive but delightful beach that is just a short stroll northwards from the bustling Padstow harbour. The meaning of the name has been lost in the mists of time, and an alternate name of 'Ship My Pumps' isn't much clearer, although it could be that ships were only allowed to pump out their bilges once past this point. A more prosaic name is Lower Beach, and it's this name that is used by the *Black Tor Ferry* and the *Rock Water Taxi* to refer to the low water embarkation point for the trip across to Rock. The likelihood is that anyone spending time on this beach will be accompanied by passengers waiting for the ferry, and there can be few more beautiful places to wait for a connection than this; the ferry runs every 20 minutes at low water.

At high water just a little strip of sand survives, inaccessible unless prepared for a swim. When the tide is fully in the water level rises to cover half the stairway and the cove becomes a natural lagoon, perfect for swimming, but don't stray out from the confines of the cove. Eventually the tide recedes sufficiently to uncover the steps down to the sand, and reveals a small beach surrounded by low cliffs that are punctuated by two small caves at the back.

The sand is golden and unblemished until a patch of shingle is revealed towards low water. Low rock outcrops are uncovered, especially beneath St Saviour's Point on the northern side where they separate the beach from St George's Cove; they are easy enough to climb over at low water. In the Middle Ages there was a chapel up on the headland dedicated to St Saviour, where a hermit tended a beacon to guide ships into the safety of the harbour. Nothing of the chapel survives but it is commemorated in the name Chapel Stile Field, where there's a huge granite cross dedicated to those lost in the two world wars. It's not a beach for rock pools but dogs are allowed all year. There's no safety equipment and it's not possible to swim at low water due to the ferry and other maritime traffic.

To find Chidley Pumps, follow the path northwards from the harbour and, after about 350yds, follow the first path to the right. It's a wonderfully sheltered spot, a Lilliputian lotus land with a tiny beach, tiny cliffs, tiny caves, and, usually, tiny waves: a classic Cornish cove in miniature.

12. ST GEORGE'S COVE
SW 919 764
DR

St George's Cove can be found about ¾ of a mile north of Padstow and consists of a relatively small inlet that at low water is transformed into a long swathe of sand, stretching from St Saviour's Point in the south to Gun Point in the north, a distance of over 800yds. The cove itself is surrounded by lush greenery, making it very sheltered apart from in easterly winds. There are lovely views across the estuary to Brea Hill and Daymer Bay and, with at least 50yds of sand above the high water mark, it's an ideal spot for a picnic or just to wait for the rest of the beach to be unveiled by the receding tide. In Victorian times the seclusion of the cove made it a favourite for the local gentry's picnics and there is a cavity cut into rocks on the Padstow side by Baptists for use in their immersion ceremonies. Today, it's a busy beach in the summer, but by low water there is plenty of room on the wide strip of soft, pale golden sand, with numerous nooks to settle in, especially towards St Saviour's Point. A small stream trickles down through the woods at the back of the cove and occasionally forms a pool above the high water mark, but more often it dries up in the sand long before reaching the sea. The beach isn't noted for rock pools but there may be an occasional one amongst the outcrops. Dog restrictions apply throughout the summer. The only access to the cove is from the Coast Path, while there are a number of paths down to the rest of the beach at low water. The nearest parking is in Padstow, where all facilities can be found.

Although the translucent waters of the estuary are very enticing, swimming is not advisable due to strong currents and the amount of maritime traffic. It may just be possible on a calm day, but only in the shallows. Safety equipment can be found at the back of the cove.

The connection with St George is based on a legend that the saint's horse 'struck its hoof' on a rock hidden somewhere in the lush woodland behind the beach, causing water to 'gush forth immediately'. There's no trace of any such well today but it could be part of the stream that trickles onto the beach. Hidden a little deeper amongst the vegetation are a few scraps of ancient walling, through which the stream runs; it's thought they may include part of a chapel, but there are certainly remnants of a boathouse and coastguard and brickmakers' cottages, and even older shipyard buildings. At the northern end of the beach, Gun Point, are remains of historical fortifications dating back to Napoleonic times, although the majority that survive today are from WW2 when they formed part of the estuary's defences against the threat of invasion. At low water it's possible, and highly recommended, to follow the beach northwards around Gun Point to the next beach, Harbour Cove.

13. HARBOUR COVE or TREGIRLS BEACH
SW 912 770
P, RP, DR

Harbour Cove, locally known as Tregirls Beach, is just over a mile from Padstow on the Coast Path, but whenever the tide allows it's more enjoyable to walk along the deliciously soft sand from St George's Cove. Passing beyond Gun Point the estuary widens out towards the open sea, while to the left the vast expanse of Tregirls is revealed: a flat sandy beach extending over 650yds in places, reaching as far as the deadly Doom Bar. It's backed for the most part by a small sand dune system, with cliffs rising gradually northwards towards Hawker's Cove; the two beaches merge as the tide recedes. The cliffs provide handy shelter from westerly winds and there may be an occasional rock pool amongst the outcrops beneath them. At high water it's a very different scenario with just a north-easterly facing thin strip of sand, some 550yds long, backed by the dunes. Dogs are allowed on the beach all year. There are breathtaking views towards Hawker's Cove, Stepper Point and Pentire Head, and across the estuary, where Daymer Bay, Bray Hill, and Brae Beach are especially prominent. Being a healthy walk from Padstow, Tregirls rarely gets busy.

Anyone unable to manage the walk from Padstow could use the seasonal field car park close to Lellizzick Farm, followed by a walk of around 250yds through attractive woodland. There is also a limited amount of roadside parking available and, whether walking from Padstow or not, there are several easy paths onto the beach. Strong estuary currents make swimming dangerous, particularly at low water; on a calm day it may be possible on a rising high tide, but only with great care and keeping within the confines of the cove. Safety equipment can be found in the dunes. The nearest facilities are in Padstow, although cream teas are available from Lellizzick Farm during the summer.

Tregirls refers to the nearby Tregirls Farm; the original name was *Tregrylls*, with the latter part being a personal name. Lellizzick derives from the Cornish *lan*, 'cell' and *losek*, 'bushy', a reference to the 6th century monastic cell founded by St Samson, who was living as a hermit. It's questionable if this is the Samson who established churches elsewhere in Cornwall and became a bishop in Brittany, but he was the saint who St Petroc first encountered after crossing the Camel. After giving Petroc his blessing, he directed him to another saint, Wethinoc, who had established a monastery nearby. The persuasive Petroc convinced Wethinoc to move elsewhere, but the monastery continued to be referred to as Lanwethinoc, thus explaining an earlier name for the town, *Lanwethenek*, 'holy place of Wethinoc'. The increasing fame of Petroc, though, wasn't to be denied and the burgeoning town eventually became *Petrocstowe*, which eventually mutated into Padstow.

In 2008, an episode of the BBC's *Time Team* was filmed in the fields directly above the beach, the team lured here by the amount of artefacts previously discovered, such as a Bronze Age axe, Iron Age round houses and pottery, Roman coins, and 5th and 6th century pottery from overseas, including Turkey and Africa. The team revealed that the cove was almost certainly the site of a harbour, something that the shifting sands of the Doom Bar would make impossible today.

14. HAWKER'S COVE
SW 912 775
P, DA

The final beach of the Camel Estuary is Hawker's Cove, which, like Tregirls, has two very different personas depending on the tide. Surprisingly, for such a remote spot, it's the site of a tiny coastal hamlet with a terrace of six cottages directly above the beach, built in 1874 for the crews of the pilot gig boats that would guide shipping around the dangerous sandbars in the estuary. Another row of cottages, about 50yds inland, was built at the turn of the 20th century to house coastguards, and there are also two former boathouses as Hawker's Cove was, from 1829, the home of the Padstow lifeboat. It may seem illogical now but the intention was for the lifeboat to be launched as close as possible to where it was most often needed, the Doom Bar, but by the 1960s the silting up of the estuary became an insurmountable problem and in 1967 a new lifeboat station was opened at Mother Ivey's Bay, some four miles to the west. On the south side of the cove is *The Old Lifeboat Station*, built in 1931 and, after the station moved, converted to a private home; the actor Edward Woodward lived there until his death in 2009, but now it's a spectacular holiday cottage.

There are no facilities here apart from *Restawhile Tea Garden,* near the coastguard cottages, serving drinks, ice creams, cream teas and small snacks throughout the summer.

At high water the small cove is flooded by the sea and the prospect of a substantial beach seems remote. Easterly facing, with fine views across the estuary to Polzeath and Daymer Bay, it's sheltered from westerly winds and as the tide begins to recede a delightfully intimate beach is revealed, mainly sand but with a few low rock outcrops at the back. It doesn't take long, though, for the beach to be transformed into a vast sweep of sand, some 600yds deep, at which point it links up with the equally stunning Tregirls to the south. Be aware that the tide comes in very quickly, and there is a channel of water, known as 'The Narrows', to the north of the cove, which varies in depth depending on the shifting sand. It's not a beach for rock pools but dogs are allowed all year.

Although it may look idyllic, the sand forms part of the notorious Doom Bar sandbank, which lurks beneath the waves when the tide is in. It's known that over 600 ships have come to grief on the Doom Bar since records began to be kept early in the 19th century. According to local folklore it was put there by a mermaid who had been shot by a local man; the tale has numerous variants, each giving a different reason why the mermaid was shot, but it's said that her cries can be heard whenever a ship grounds on the sandbar. Even today, despite regular dredging and improvements in navigational technology, vessels can still come to grief on it.

Swimming is only advisable within the narrow cove itself on a rising high tide - it's dangerous at all other times. There is no safety equipment. Kite surfers can sometimes be seen in the bay shared with Tregirls, but it's not suitable for beginners or for surfing. It's best to park on the road approaching Lellizzick Farm and then follow the road leading directly down to the cove; otherwise use the same seasonal field car park as used for Tregirls, when it's best to take the path to that beach and follow the Coast Path to the hamlet, a total distance of about half a mile. There's easy access to the beach via a slipway. Despite its beauty, Hawker's Cove never really gets crowded. This is partly due to the limited parking and isolated location, but also because of the alluring ribbon of sand between here and the tourist hotspot of Padstow. Comparatively few people make it this far, but those that do are amply rewarded.

15. TREVONE - PORTHMISSEN BEACH
SW 891 759
P, RP, SF, SW, L, DR

After leaving the sheltered gentility of the Camel Estuary we embark upon a journey along the rugged, sea-battered coast that makes up the bulk of this guide. We begin at Trevone Bay, roughly two miles west of Padstow, where there are two contrasting beaches, the gloriously sandy Porthmissen, usually referred to as Trevone Beach, and Newtrain Bay, which lives up to its local nickname of Rocky Beach.

Porthmissen is a typical inlet beach, being much deeper than it is wide, with sand at all stages of the tide. At high water it's around 50yds deep, but extends to 350yds at low water, and for the most part it's roughly 150yds wide, bounded by cliffs, until around mid-tide when a vast rocky reef is exposed on the western side; at low water it's possible to scramble over the rocks to Newtrain Bay. It's a gently shelving beach of pale golden sand, with a few sheltered nooks carved into the cliffs on the western side providing some seclusion from the summer hordes. There are a couple of small rock stacks and a rocky reef exposed towards the centre of the beach by the receding tide, perfect for climbing and the site of an occasional rock pool – more pools can be found in the reef on the western side. A small stream enters from the back of the beach but quickly disperses across the sand. Dog restrictions apply during the summer. The name comes from *porth mesen,* 'acorn port', and traces of a submerged oak forest can sometimes be seen at low water, especially after winter storms.

37

The gently sloping sand will tempt many into the sea but swimming should only be undertaken with care due to strong rip currents, particularly on the eastern side of the beach; it's better to swim only in the area designated as safe by the RNLI Lifeguards, who patrol in the summer. Surfing is good from low to mid-tide when it's suitable for intermediate and experienced surfers. There are two lots of safety equipment.

There's easy access from two good-sized car parks, although they are often full during the summer, and there's a little roadside parking just above the beach. The one road in and out of the village is often congested at peak times, but bus users have no option other than to follow it for around ¾ of a mile from the nearest bus stop, Trevone Turn, on the B3276. In the left hand car park there's a café with an outdoor seating area, a beach shop and a surf shop, where equipment can be hired or bought. Public toilets are nearby and, just above the beach, there's a grassy field providing fine views of the bay. Unlike many coastal villages, Trevone has a thriving local community and throughout the summer there are numerous village fetes and activities, at which all are welcome. There's a shop selling local produce and a range of gifts, and an inn, *The Well Parc Hotel.*

Trevone is best known for its menacing Round Hole, a collapsed sea cave on the cliffs to the east. At high tide, but only on a calm day, it's possible to kayak right though the channel that connects to the sea. Take care if going to view the hole as there have been numerous reports of people having to be rescued after tumbling 80ft to the bottom.

It was only after the arrival of the railways into Cornwall that Trevone began to develop as a tourist centre; before that it was an isolated farming community, and its beach the preserve of fishermen and, on dark, moonless nights, smugglers. In 1765, William Rawlings, a resident of Padstow, informed the Earl of Dartmouth that his servants had encountered no less than 60 horses laden with cargo on a beach two miles west of Padstow: Porthmissen. According to Rawlings, each horse had "three bags of tea on them of 56 or 58lbs weight" and, as that is unlikely to have been an isolated event, it's clear that this sheltered and isolated beach was put to good use by the smuggling fraternity. Today, that same beach is a perfect location for family holidays and its unspoilt beauty worth seeing at any time of the year.

16. TREVONE - NEWTRAIN BAY
SW 886 756
P, RP, SW, DA

At low water it's possible to reach the second Trevone beach, Newtrain Bay, directly from Porthmissen by an adventurous scramble over the rocky outcrops that lie beneath the small promontory called Pentonwarra Point, but it's easier to take a short walk along the Coast Path from the westerly car park until a slipway leads down to the beach. There are also several paths to the rocky shore further to the west. It's a wide beach of rock platforms, outcrops, and gullies housing a multitude of delightful and varying rock pools. There are some patches of shingle and sand, the latter found mainly at the western end. It's almost completely covered at high water and tends to be more exposed than Porthmissen, but it's always quieter than its sandy neighbour. Dogs are allowed on Newtrain throughout the year, while all facilities can be found in Trevone.

One of the delightful features of the beach is a good-sized sea water pool that has been created amongst the rocks. It's known as 'Tinker Bunny's Bathing Pool' after a tinker who lived on the cliff above the pool. It's believed that he was the son of a Padstow clockmaker and there is a census record of a John Bonney, or Boney, a clockmaker, living in Padstow in the mid-19th century. Perhaps Tinker helped to create the pool, or maybe he was just a frequent bather. Swimming in the crystal clear water of the pool is a delight, but it's not advisable to swim anywhere else on the beach due to strong currents. There is no safety equipment.

On 20th December 1924 a Yarmouth steam trawler, *Smilin' Thro'*, was blown onto the rocks and wrecked during a severe storm. Thankfully there was no loss of life as the crew were able to clamber down and walk to safety, but fish was definitely on the Christmas menu for many locals that year. The remains of the wreck can sometimes be seen at low water.

There's a legend that piskies used to hold dances at night on the cliffs above the bay; they danced so often that the grass was worn away and their tiny footprints were clearly visible until the friable cliffs were undermined and broken down by the relentless sea.

The rock pools of Newtrain Bay are a source of delight for people of all ages and there are some basic tips for getting the most out of the experience: The lower the tide, the more pools there will be; start with the pools closest to the sea and work your way back up the shore. Use a bucket or plastic container as a scoop rather than using a net, which can cause damage to small creatures. Don't wade into the pool as this can also cause damage - stand or kneel on the edge. Carefully replace rocks or stones after looking under them, and always gently return sea creatures to where you found them, ensuring they are the right way up.

Trevone is one of the bays included in a longstanding marketing campaign, *7 Bays for 7 Days*, the others being Harlyn, Mother Ivey's, Booby's, Constantine, Treyarnon and Porthcothan. The rocky shore of Newtrain makes a delightful contrast to the other beaches and, in combination with the sandy shore of Porthmissen, it's certainly easy to spend an enjoyable day at Trevone.

17. HARLYN BAY
SW 878 754
P, PT, RP, SF, SW, L, DA

Separated from Newtrain Bay by St Cadoc's Point, Harlyn Bay is a crescent-shaped sweep of glorious golden sand, consisting of the main northerly facing Harlyn Beach and a number of small coves that link up at low water. At high water, Harlyn Beach has a fair sized strip of sand, and as the tide ebbs it's soon possible to reach the smaller Bloodhound Cove and the even smaller Greenclose Cove. At low water the length of the three beaches combined is some 700yds, with the tide retreating to a depth of 350yds. Beyond Greenclose is the next beach, Onjohn Cove, separated by a low reef of rock outcrops but accessible through the rocks at most low tides. The sand is mainly broken sea shells, with a calcium carbonate concentrate of over 80%, making it popular as a fertilizer and for many years farmers took away cartloads from above the high water mark for spreading on their fields. The beach is often split by a stream that crosses it, but the course of the stream frequently changes and in summer the build up of sand can be such that it virtually disappears. The bay is sumptuously sandy for most of the summer but in winter there can be patches of shingle. Much of the south-eastern part of the bay is backed by low sand dunes but it becomes rockier to the west. The rock outcrops to the north around St Cadoc's Point are accessible and house numerous rock pools. St Cadoc was a 6th century Welsh abbot.

The sand dunes give way to low cliffs at Bloodhound Cove, providing a little more shelter. It tends to be slightly quieter than the main beach and is accessible from the Coast Path by a flight of steps. It's named after HMS *Bloodhound*, wrecked here on 16th December 1811 when Lt Josias Bray tragically mistook Trevose Head for Stepper Point, resulting in the drowning of 11 men. Greenclose Cove is even more secluded and sheltered but the area of sand above the high water mark is small and cut off at high water, so it's important to keep an eye on the incoming tide. There are fine views of Gulland Rock on the horizon; it was once used for target practice by planes from Royal Naval Air Station based at St Merryn, when a large white circle was painted on its cliffs.

Dogs are allowed all year and the beach is cleaned regularly during the summer. Harlyn is extremely popular, particularly with the patrons of the numerous caravan and camp sites in the area. There's easy access from the large car park that overlooks the main beach, with a seasonal kiosk café and public toilets found in the grassy overflow car park. There's also a beach shop, bar and restaurant at *The Harlyn Inn*, on the road close to the beach. The Padstow to Newquay bus stops at Harlyn Bridge by the entrance to the beach.

The original name was *Perleze Bay*, 'grey or blue landing place', while the modern name comes from the Cornish *Ar-Lyn*, 'facing a lake', a reference to the calm waters found in the sheltered bay, conditions which make Harlyn one of the safer beaches for swimming, especially on a calm day on a rising high tide. It is still, however, safest when RNLI Lifeguards patrol during the summer, and be aware that strong, unpredictable currents make it dangerous at low water. Surfing is good, but the shelter provided by Trevose Head generally makes it more attractive for beginners than experts, with *Harlyn Surf School* providing lessons from the beach, plus lessons in SUP and sea kayaking. Safety equipment can be found above the beach.

The history of human activity at Harlyn goes back thousands of years and there have been multiple archaeological discoveries here. In 1900 a large Iron Age cemetery with over 200 graves was uncovered during the digging of foundations for a house near to the beach. All the bodies were buried in slate coffins, knees to chin, and with skulls fractured to allow their souls to find freedom. In 1990 an early Bronze Age burial pit was discovered, including a pottery vessel containing a bronze pendant as well as cremated human and animal remains, while severe storms in 2014 unearthed more human remains in the friable cliffs. Meanwhile, in 1581, Anne Piers, the mother of a Padstow sea captain turned notorious pirate, John Piers, was accused of witchcraft and receiving stolen goods; she was found not guilty of witchcraft – using her dark arts to help her son – but guilty of the latter charge. It was said that "Piers hathe conveyed all such goods and spoiles as he hathe wickedlie gotten at the seas" to his mother, who then hid much of the loot in the cliffs at Harlyn Bay.

Voted as one of the top 10 beaches in the UK for families and activities, Harlyn is spacious enough to cope with the summer crowds, especially as most visitors tend to congregate at the car park end, or even on the car park itself with its panoramic view of the bay. In an area blessed with an abundance of wonderful beaches it has the variety, beauty and history to fully warrant its popularity and should certainly be visited by all beach lovers.

18. ONJOHN COVE - BOAT COVE
SW 872 758
RP, SW, DA

The enigmatically named Onjohn Cove lies on the west side of Harlyn Bay and is split into two small beaches, Cellars Cove to the north and Boat Cove to the south. Boat Cove is just over half a mile from the car park at Harlyn and is accessed from the Coast Path by a path and stone slipway. Access is also possible over the low rock outcrops from Greenclose Cove at most low tides, and more outcrops to the north can be scrambled over to reach Cellars Cove.

There's usually a small area of sand above the high watermark and by low water the beach can extend to 140yds in depth, surrounded by rock outcrops and low, friable cliffs. Beneath the cliffs is a breeze-block storage shed with safety equipment mounted on it. It's more sheltered than Harlyn beach but tends to be the busier of the two Onjohn beaches, partly due to its accessibility from the main beach, but also because of its obvious accessibility and the alluring view of it from the Coast Path. Dogs are allowed on the beach and there are usually rocks pools amongst the outcrops, especially to the north.

Both Onjohn beaches are less affected by swell and surf than their neighbours to the east, so swimming is fine on calm days on a rising tide, but not advisable at low water. There is safety equipment, but the RNLI Lifeguards who patrol Harlyn are likely to be preoccupied by the activity on the main beach.

In 1865 a labourer discovered a pot containing an axe and what he thought were 'two bits of brass' on the cliff above the beach. He used the 'bits of brass' to hold his trousers up until his boss spotted them and suggested they should be examined by an expert. They were found to be two wafer-thin crescents of gold known as lunulae, dating from the early Bronze Age (2300-2000 BC), and were probably deposited as grave goods as there are several prehistoric burial mounds nearby. They would have been worn around the neck like a collar but were clearly too fine for ordinary everyday wear, and their shape, resembling the crescent moon, suggests a symbolic meaning, making it likely they were objects of great ritual and ceremonial significance. One of the lunulae appears to have come from Ireland, while the decoration on the other is similar to that found on five lunulae discovered in Brittany, suggesting they were the work of one craftsman who either worked or traded on both sides of the Channel.

19. ONJOHN COVE - CELLARS COVE
SW 872 759
RP, SW, DA

The northerly part of Onjohn Cove is Cellars Cove, named after the 400 year old house above the beach, now known as *The Cellars*, a luxurious holiday home that sleeps 13 people, but was once a pilchard pressing 'cellar' with two single-storied wings at the rear in which pilchards were salted and stored. Carved into a granite lintel are the words *Lucri Dulcis Odor*, 'Profit Smells Sweet', and back in the 16th century the owner of the cottage ran a lucrative business from here, exporting pilchards to countries like Italy, where they were very popular. By the 1870s the bay was a hive of activity with several pilchard seine companies operating from the beaches, while at the same time impoverished villagers were struggling to make ends meet. One day, when a shipment of pilchards was returned from Italy unsold, the starving villagers asked the owner if they could have the fish, even though they were now well past their best. Selfishly, the owner turned them down and decided to plough the pilchards into a field as fertilizer, causing the villagers' spokeswoman, a local white witch or wise woman called Mother Ivey, to put a curse on the field so that 'if ever its soil was broken, death would follow'. At first, the business continued to use the field but it wasn't long before the curse claimed its first victim when the eldest son was thrown from his horse and killed while riding in the field. It went on to be associated with an unusually high death toll and in 1997 South West Water, in preparation for laying a pipe in the field, enlisted the help of the vicar of St Columb to lift the curse. Some accounts suggest the curse extended to the owner, his family, and even the cottage, but the latter may have been tagged on in 2008 when the then future Prime Minister David Cameron stayed there with his family; Mr Cameron, of course, ignominiously resigned following the Brexit referendum in 2016. An additional twist was added to the cottage's grisly past when, during renovations in the last century, hidden staircases and rooms featuring 'grim evidence of torture' were discovered.

Thankfully, no curse has been cast on the small but delightful beach at Cellars Cove. Surrounded by moderately high cliffs, it consists of perhaps 30yds of golden sand leading to an area of rock platforms and outcrops, interspersed with more sand. A small tunnel leads to a further area of outcrops and sand to the south, and at low water it's possible to cross over to Boat Cove. Dogs are allowed and there are usually a few rock pools amongst the outcrops. The beach is virtually covered at high water. The nearest facilities and parking are at Harlyn.

Sheltering in the lee of Cataclews Point (*carrek loos*, 'grey rock'), there is very little swell, making it suitable for swimming in calm weather on an incoming high tide, but unsuitable for surfing. Swimming should be avoided at low water. Some good snorkelling can be found to the north, especially around Big Guns Cove, where there's another small beach that is now inaccessible from land due to cliff falls. There is no safety equipment and the lifeguards on Harlyn Beach don't patrol this far.

Hidden beneath the cliffs, Cellars Cove is by far the quietest beach in the bay, possibly due to the small gate that guards the path down the cliff; it also carries a warning about unstable cliffs, and it certainly isn't advisable to sit beneath them. A slipway provides easy access to the sand. There's a small boathouse at the top of the slipway; a local fisherman has permission to launch his boat from the beach.

20. MOTHER IVEY'S BAY
SW 864 759
SW, DA

Mother Ivey is the local wise-woman or white witch we encountered at Onjohn Cove. As she showed in that incident, she was a vocal member of the community who used her charms and knowledge to right any wrongs and sort out disputes. How much truth there is in the legends associated with her isn't clear, but there certainly was an Ivey family living in the parish in the 17th and 18th centuries, including at least three named Martha – could Mother Ivey have been one of those? One of the prominent features of the beach is Mother Ivey's Cottage, which overlooks Little Cove. It's unclear whether she actually lived there but it was once a pilchard cellar; an auction for the 'Mother Ive Pilchard Fishery' was held on 30th September 1879, the sale including a 'nearly new, stone-built, slate-covered fish cellar with 19 sleeping-berths, two seines, two seine-boats, about 30 oars, horses, 40 pilchard hogsheads, and 170 tons of French salt'. The reserve price of £490 was not met. More recently the cottage garden and the beach were used as some of the main backdrops for filming Rosamund Pilcher's *Four Seasons*, featuring Tom Conti, Michael Yorke, Frank Findley and Senta Berger. The Cornish name is Polventon Bay, from *Poll Fenten*, 'cove of a spring', but it's barely used today, with the common name dating back to at least the late 1800s.

The bay lies between Cataclews Point and Merrope Rocks on the sheltered side of Trevose Head and consists of a number of small coves, of which only one, Little Cove, has sand at all stages of the tide. Making up the eastern end of the beach, Little Cove is also the site of the main access

48

path, with the only other access via a steeper path close to Mother Ivey's Cottage. It has sand at all stages of the tide, being around 100yds wide at high water. There are a number of other more secluded sandy areas to the north, with Long Cove being the largest, although this can only be reached at very low tides, and if venturing onto any of the coves it's important to keep an eye on the tide and be close to the access points before high water. All together it's about 500yds wide at low water.

Dogs are allowed on the beach, but it's not noted for rock pools although there may be an odd one amongst the rocky outcrops on the north-eastern side of Little Cove. There are regular beach cleans organised by the holiday park situated on the cliffs above the beach. The nearest car park is a seasonal one shared with Booby's Bay, in a field, with a walk of over 600yds to the nearest access point. Apart from this the nearest parking is at Trevose Head or Harlyn Bay, both with longer, but thrilling, walks to the beach. There are no facilities unless staying at the holiday park, the nearest being at Harlyn Bay or Constantine. This lack of parking and facilities causes Mother Ivey's to be virtually deserted throughout the off-season, but the patrons of the holiday park ensure it's busy during the summer.

Swimming is fine on an incoming tide, but don't stray too far from shore because there are strong currents in the deeper water. There can be some interesting snorkelling around Long Cove at high water. It's not a surfing beach and there's no safety equipment.

The other prominent feature of the bay is the spectacularly situated Padstow Lifeboat House. Constructed in 2006, it benefits from additional shelter provided by the Merope Rocks on the western end of the bay, and houses the Tamar class lifeboat, *Spirit of Padstow*. The station is open to visitors from Monday to Friday most weeks. Exercise launches also take place every week, operational requirements permitting.

21. BOOBY'S BAY
SW 857 754
P, RP, SF, L, DA

Booby's Bay lies on the exposed western side of the Trevose Head Heritage Coast, an unspoilt, often windswept stretch of coastline with high, rugged cliffs that provide important sites for a number of breeding seabirds including fulmars, razorbills, and guillemots. Booby's takes its name from another seabird found in the area, a close relative of the gannet. From the headland, with its lighthouse built in 1847, the view encompasses almost the whole of the north Cornish coast, from Hartland Point in Devon to Pendeen Watch, but after the neighbouring Dinas Head the cliffs gradually decrease in height, the turf becomes deliciously springy underfoot and the views of the forthcoming beaches unsurpassed. In such a bucolic area there's something incongruous about the four detached houses perched on the low cliffs above the bay, but we should be thankful that a pre-WW2 plan to build a housing estate there never came to fruition. Those cliffs surround Booby's Bay, which is separated from the neighbouring Constantine Bay by a low rocky reef and the diminutive, grass-crowned Constantine Island. It's a beautiful beach of light golden sand, fringed by rock outcrops and platforms that need to be negotiated in order to reach the sand; there are some obvious and easy routes but many visitors choose to walk along the sand from Constantine Beach. At high water just a few rock platforms and perhaps an occasional patch of shingle survive, but by low water it stretches to a length of 600yds and a depth of around 300yds, including the outcrops. A number of nooks and inlets provide shelter, depending on the wind direction, and there are plenty of fascinating rock pools to explore, including some large enough to paddle in. Dogs are allowed all year.

Being westerly facing, Booby's is exposed to the prevailing wind and bears the brunt of the Atlantic swell and, with rip currents and submerged rocks posing additional dangers, swimming should definitely not be attempted other than when RNLI Lifeguards are present during the summer, in the area they designate as safe. The strong swell and surf combine with the beach profile to make it one of Cornwall's more challenging surfing spots, and a favourite for experienced surfers, but the conditions are definitely too dangerous for everyone else, especially beginners. There is safety equipment at the back of the beach.

At low water the wreck of SV *Carl* of Hamburg can sometimes be seen; the ship had been impounded at the start of WW1 and in October 1917 was being towed to London to be broken up for scrap, when she broke free in a storm and ran aground on the beach. The fierce storms of February 2014 saw giant waves strip away almost 3ft of sand, revealing much more than usual of the 60ft vessel in its final resting place.

On the cliffs at the southern end of the beach is a small stone and slate cottage known as Tom Parson's Hut. Now owned by the National Trust, but not open to the public, it was the home of a notorious smuggler and 'wrecker' of that name. The 1841 census lists the occupant as Thomas Parsons, farmer, along with his wife, Elizabeth, and three children. Legend suggests he used the notorious method of tying a lantern to a donkey's tail before leading it along the low cliffs and dunes to simulate the lights of a port, thus luring unsuspecting ships to their doom. It's a colourful tale but there's no record of any such activity taking place in Cornwall and it's inconceivable that a mainly maritime community would have tolerated it. It's likely that he supplemented his farming income with a bit of smuggling and more traditional wrecking, the looting of ships wrecked along the coast, which was seen as the 'bounty of the sea' by the Cornish.

There are no facilities at all at Booby's Bay, the nearest refreshments and toilets being at Constantine, while there is a seasonal car park in a field just over 300yds inland and small car parks at Trevose Head and Constantine, and a larger one at Treyarnon Bay. The nearest bus stop is by *Constantine Surf Shop* in the centre of the village. The lack of facilities and tricky access make Booby's the least family-friendly of the *7 Bays for 7 Days*, but anyone who takes the trouble to visit will find another fantastic beach that is well worth seeking out.

22. CONSTANTINE BAY
SW 858 748
P, PT, RP, SF, L, DA

Separated from Booby's Bay by a narrow, rocky reef, Constantine Bay is a gently curving, west facing beach, backed by masses of marram-covered dunes, some of which now house *Trevose Golf Club*. The beach is conveniently split into two sections with the northern, larger area consisting of flat golden sand that links up with Booby's at low water, while to the south there's a wide rocky shelf that continues beyond Treyarnon Point and is home to dozens of delightful rock pools. This area is backed by a seawall, originally constructed in the 1940s. The two areas combine to a length of 800yds, but at high water there's just a narrow, but lengthy, strip of sand. A stream meanders across the centre of the beach, while midway along the rocky reef is Chair Cove, a small sandy patch amongst the rocks which is usually deserted, but be aware of the returning tide if visiting.

There's less sand on the beach after storms when patches of stones can be uncovered at low tide. Dogs are allowed all year. The only caveat is that it is quite exposed and there are few sheltered spots on windy days, but otherwise it's a perfect beach for families, and very popular during the summer, partly due to the plethora of holiday camps nearby. There's easy access via a ramp or steps, and two car parks, a large seasonal one about 270yds away, and a small all year one just above the beach, but this is usually full during the summer. Some people choose to park at Treyarnon

Bay and walk along the Coast Path from there. Public toilets can be found by the small car park. Just above the beach, *Coastal Coffee* serves drinks and snacks from a van, and there's usually an ice-cream van present. There's a shop for general provisions in the village, with the nearest bus stop nearby, a 900yd walk from the beach.

Constantine is regarded as one of Cornwall's best surfing beaches as it receives the full force of the Atlantic swell, fine for experts but not great for the inexperienced. Luckily, *Constantine Bay Surf School* are on hand to provide lessons. Strong rip currents make swimming dangerous and it's advisable to swim only when RNLI Lifeguards are present during the summer, keeping to the area they designate as safe. Safety equipment is situated by the northern access point and the lifeguard hut.

The bay is named after a 6th century Cornish king and martyr, and there's a narrow, sunken footpath through the dunes to a holy well and medieval church dedicated to him, now on the golf course. The sand dunes support an increasing population of the White Sandhill Snail; it's believed to be the only known site in England for this species. Fences and marram grass have been installed to prevent erosion as at one time the dunes were much higher. During WW2 the whole area was a minefield and, even after the mines were supposedly removed at the end of the war, a number of unfortunate dogs were blown to pieces after stepping on one that had been missed. The small, grass covered Constantine Island, situated amongst the outcrops that separate the beach from Booby's Bay, is the site of a Bronze Age barrow, discovered in 2007 when the skeleton of an adult male was unearthed in a cist, a small stone-lined box, on the seaward side of the island. It was found on top of a sandy mound that contained bones from at least 4 other bodies, while a piece of Neolithic pottery was located below the mound and Mesolithic flints were also found in the area.

23. TREYARNON BAY
SW 858 739
P, RP, SF, SW, L, DA

On a coastline decorated with an abundance of glorious sandy beaches, we arrive at another gem, Treyarnon Bay, an inlet beach bounded by Treyarnon Point to the north and Trethias Island to the south. Backed by a small area of sand dunes and surrounded by low cliffs, there's sand at all stages of the tide but with a huge variation between high, 50yds, and low, more than 400yds, while the bay is around 200yds at its widest. It's a north-westerly facing, flat beach consisting of soft, golden sand bisected by a shallow stream, with a number of small inlets accessible as the tide recedes, including Well Cove and Long Cove on the north side and Benges Cove on the south; they provide additional shelter depending on the wind direction. Dogs are allowed all year. To the north of Well Cove there's a swimming pool in the rocks, a natural hollow that has been dammed at one end and is filled with sea water by the incoming tide. At 100ft long it's big enough for serious swimmers as well as those who just want to splash around or search for starfish and crabs. The rocky reef on the northern side of the beach contains a vast array of pools that can be explored. On the south side, where the cliffs are higher, are numerous outcrops, perfect for childhood adventures, including Trethias Island, topped with thrift and thick, springy grass and home to breeding sea birds. The island is separated from the headland by a deep, steep gulley which can be explored at low water, apart from neap tides when it remains under water. At the end of the gulley, on the left, there is

54

a small square opening leading to a large cave which extends through the headland and emerges into the cove adjacent to Treyarnon, Wine Cove, a name redolent of the smugglers who landed their illicit bounty there and in the neighbouring Pepper Cove. Please note that the cave is only accessible at low water, and at least some of it is likely to be flooded - it's more suitable for coasteering! The tide rushes in around the island, so any exploration of this area should only be undertaken on an ebbing tide, and allow plenty of time to be back on the main beach.

Treyarnon is another beach where swimming is only safe when RNLI Lifeguards are present during the summer, keeping to the area they designate as suitable. Rip currents and submerged rocks make it hazardous at all other times, with the possible exception of a rising high tide on a very calm day, but it's safer to keep to the swimming pool. Safety equipment can be found above the beach. It's a very popular surfing beach and suitable for all levels of experience, including beginners. Experienced surfers tend to favour the southern side, although most of them head for Constantine or Booby's.

There's a large car park next to the beach with easy access provided by a slipway. The bus stops at Treyarnon Turn on the B3276 but it may be more enjoyable to get off at Constantine and follow the Coast Path from that beach. Public toilets are situated on the northerly cliffs, and a seasonal beach shop and refreshments are available in the car park, while the Youth Hostel, also on the northerly cliffs, has the popular *Trey Bay Café* with an outdoor seating area.

The name comes from *Tre Arnen*, 'farm of Yarnen'. In 1831 the body of a young man enclosed in a case was washed up on the beach. The corpse was buried on the cliffs and it was soon discovered that he was a cholera victim, so all those who handled the body were put under quarantine. In 1899 a large steamship moored in the bay before launching a small boat containing three stowaways who'd been caught when hunger forced them to break cover on the ship. Once onshore they headed for Falmouth, perhaps to steal onboard another ship, while the steamship continued to the Canary Islands.

Treyarnon has been recommended by the Marine Conservation Society's Good Beach Guide as one of the best family beaches in the area and it's deservedly very popular, having all that is needed for a perfect holiday, plus the cave, island, and bathing pool for the more adventurous.

24. PORTHCOTHAN
SW 857 720
P, PT. RP. SF, SW, L, DA

Porthcothan is the last of the *7 Bays for 7 Days* on our journey and is proof, if any is needed, that the marketing campaign really doesn't lie: it actually is possible to spend a full day at each of these wonderful beaches. The protection of the National Trust has allowed Porthcothan to stay relatively unchanged: there's a straggle of houses, mainly of pre-WW2 construction with later redevelopments, on the southern cliffs but the north side is completely unblemished. The excellent shop, selling general provisions as well as beach equipment and refreshments, is neatly tucked away on the southern side, and the car park, big enough for 175 cars, is hidden out of sight on the other side of the B3276. Public toilets are also situated in the car park. The bus stop is right next to the beach and there are two easy access paths, but anyone arriving at high water, when there is only about 30yds of sand crammed into a narrow cove, could be fooled into thinking this is an ordinary beach. It's only as the tide recedes that the full majesty of Porthcothan is unveiled because it's a classic inlet beach, with the tide retreating a remarkable 600yds, while the narrow cove becomes almost triangular in shape as it opens up to link with Long Cove to the north and Golden Burn to the south, a distance of over 400yds.

The beach consists of pale golden sand fringed with jagged rocks and flanked by cliffs that have been carved by the sea into wonderfully grotesque shapes. It's backed by a small sand dune system through which a stream flows onto the beach, meandering along the north side before dispersing, but periodically diverting to run along the toe of the dunes, which are high, hummocky, and well vegetated with grasses and brambles. The cliffs make it a well-sheltered beach with the small inlet of Totty Cove, on the northern side, providing additional shelter, as does the fantastically shaped Long Cove. To the south the beach links up with Golden Burn, another sheltered spot with caves to explore and outcrops to climb. Golden Burn has separate access from the Coast Path and a small patch of sand at high water when it is cut off from the main beach. Huge rock stacks abound, framing the beautiful views across to Trevose Head, but one of the most picturesque rocks, an arched formation known as Jan

Leverton's Rock, was destroyed when the beach was pounded by 30ft waves and 70mph winds during the storms of 2014. There are plenty of rock pools amongst the stacks and outcrops on both flanks, while dogs are allowed all year.

RNLI Lifeguards patrol the beach during the summer and it's only safe to swim when they are present; submerged rocks and rip currents make it dangerous at other times, although it may be possible on a calm day on an incoming high tide. Surfing is fine for beginners and those of intermediate level, but the shelter provided by the offshore islets, grandly known as the Trescore Islands, makes it insufficiently testing for experienced surfers. The islands create a lagoon between themselves and the mainland and at low spring tides it's possible to scramble down from the Coast-Path and swim across to them; there's usually the bonus of an additional small sandy beach. It's also possible to swim from Golden Burn on calm days but this should only be considered with extreme care. Safety equipment can be found at the back of the main beach and Golden Burn.

The meaning of the name is unclear but one translations suggests 'cove with the hidden landing place', which would be appropriate as Porthcothan was a favourite smuggling cove and the huge stack off the northern headland is called Wills' Rock, named after a customs officer, Tom Wills, who used it as a convenient perch from where he could keep an eye on the surrounding coves. One night he surprised a gang bringing goods ashore, but they retaliated by tying him up and leaving him to drown. Amazingly, and showing great tenacity, he escaped by rolling over and over to beyond the high water mark where he was eventually spotted and freed.

Cornwall's greatest playwright, Nick Darke, lived for many years, until his death in 2005, in one of the houses above the beach. Much of his work evoked the spirit of Cornwall, but there was far more to him than just writing: he was also a fisherman, beachcomber, environmentalist, politician, and film-maker. One of his films, *The Wrecking Season,* made with his wife, Anne, was about 'wrecking', the practice of gathering items washed up on the beach, often, in times past, from wrecked ships. In February 2014 much of Porthcothan beach was strewn with debris from *Le Sillon*, a French trawler wrecked on rocks at Totty Cove, just over a ½ mile away – all the crew were rescued. People came from miles around to gather the 'harvest of the sea', as it is traditionally called in Cornwall, which included plastic crates, boxes of fish, and even small bits from the wreck itself, forcing the Coastguard Agency to issue a warning that all items taken had to be reported – failure to do so would result in a heavy fine. This was a modern version of the age old argument about the ownership of 'wrecked' goods.

Porthcothan's beauty has long been recognised and it's no surprise to learn that it features in the BBC adaptation of Poldark, with the landward side doubling as Nampara Cove and the seaward side as Hendrawna Beach. While it's an exaggeration to call it a 'secret' beach, it is usually considerably quieter than the other *7 Bays*, perhaps because it's further from the tourist hot-spot of Padstow, but it's a magnificent beach that should definitely be near the top of any 'must see' list.

25. PORTH MEAR
SW 849 714
RP, SW, DA

Porth Mear is just half a mile from Golden Burn at Porthcothan but its rocky shore provides a complete contrast to the magnificent sandy beaches that make up the *7 Bays*. It's another inlet beach, nestling at the end of a graceful green valley, and it's possible to follow a permissive path down the valley from the small car park at Pentire Farm (Park Head). A stream runs through the valley and onto the beach, close to the path which allows easy access to the patch of shingle and grey sand that makes up the back of the beach. From there on, apart from an occasional patch of sand, it's virtually all low rock platforms, home to a ream of rock pools, and it's the latter that make Porth Mear such a special spot.

The beach is sheltered from all but northerly winds and the surrounding grassy cliffs are ideal for picnics or waiting for the tide to recede. At high water only the shingle area survives but the ebbing tide quickly reveals the rock platforms that run right to the mouth of the inlet. The Cornish phrase *An Bollenessor* means 'the rock pool hunter' and this beach would be paradise for the most avid of them. There's a huge variation in the size and depth of the pools and they contain a multitude of brightly coloured seaweed and fascinating creatures, with usually lots of fish, some living in the pools, others becoming trapped as the tide falls. Notable are the Cornish clingfish that attach to the rocks using a sucker on their belly – they're easily recognised by their duck-bill shaped face and the two iridescent blue spots on top of their head. Large rock gobies and corkwing wrasse can be found in the deeper pools, while scorpion fish might be spotted lurking among the rocks. Overhanging rocks are ideal for cushion stars and the Celtic sea slug, while the seaweed-packed pools provide perfect conditions for sea hares to spawn: look out for their pink spaghetti eggs, but be aware that sea hares squirt out purple ink when threatened. There are many species of crab, including the tiny porcelain crab, green shore crab, and hermit crab, which have yellow eyes and a right claw much bigger than the left. Most precious of all is the St Piran's hermit crab, which after an absence of more than 30 years began to reappear around Cornwall in 2016. It's thought that the loss of this species owed much to pollution from the *Torrey Canyon* disaster in 1967 when much of its cargo of oil ended up on the Cornish coast. The oil, along with huge quantities of solvent emulsifying chemicals used in an attempt to disperse it, decimated seabird populations and marine wildlife. Concerned by the impact on his local beach, Porth Mear, a biology teacher, Richard Pearce, then aged 26, decided to monitor the environmental impact. He's repeated the exercise three times a year ever since, creating a remarkable five decade record of nature's resilience against a man-made disaster. He found the beach was barren for five years before seaweeds began to flourish on rocks that had been stripped bare by chemicals, and it took around 10 years for the beach to return to something like normality. In an era when global warming and man-made pollution threaten our shore wildlife more than ever, Richard's survey provides an invaluable conservation tool with its wealth of data about the seashore and how it changes. As for the St Piran's crab, its existence remains precarious but it seems to be slowly recovering. It favours pools containing pink coralline seaweed, has equal sized claws, bright red hairy legs, long red eye stalks and black eyes with white spots, the latter providing the inspiration for its common name, the colours being the same as St Piran's flag.

 Despite there being no safety equipment, swimming and snorkelling are fine within the inlet on a calm day when the tide is sufficiently high, but it's not safe at low water because of currents and submerged rocks. It's not a surfing beach. Dogs are allowed, but there are no facilities, the nearest being at Porthcothan.

26. PENTIRE STEPS BEACH
SW 847 703
P, DA

The beautiful Pentire Steps sits at the remote northern end of the famous Bedruthan Steps, beyond Diggory's Island, the last of the gigantic rock stacks so beloved by photographers. Backed by huge, precipitous cliffs, there's no beach at high water but the ebbing tide reveals a horseshoe shaped cove which extends northwards at low water, the pristine golden sand broken only by one large outcrop in the centre. The sea-battered cliffs are prone to crumbling and the sand is fringed with fallen boulders, while the grass-topped Diggory's Island forms a barrier that few of Bedruthan's visitors choose to pass. It's a beach for sand pools rather than rock pools, while many of the outcrops that separate the main part of the beach from the northern extension are encrusted with mussels. On a calm, sunny day the aquamarine sea looks tempting but this is not a place for swimming: powerful rip currents and fast moving tides make it extremely dangerous at all times. It is, though, a favourite secret spot for experienced surfers, but all other levels shouldn't even consider it. There is no safety equipment.

Access to the beach is not for the fainthearted, the Victorian steps featured in the name having been washed away in the 1960s and early 1970s. Nowadays there are two obvious tracks from the top of the cliffs but the seaward one has crumbled away about halfway down, while the other requires a head for heights and is for the nimble-footed only, needing climbing and scrambling skills at the lower end. Despite this it is regularly used by surfers who, sherpa-like, make the descent look easy despite having to carry their boards, so it might be a good idea to follow one of them down to the beach. Happily, for those who don't fancy that precarious route, there is direct access from Bedruthan beach from around an hour before low water, when it's possible to scramble over the rocks between the cliffs and Diggory's Island or through an archway in the island, which more than likely involves paddling through a sand pool. A short while before that it is possible, on a calm day, to paddle through the shallows between the beaches, which some might find a delightful finish to an awe-inspiring walk. Choose as low a tide as possible - spring tides are best – making it feasible to have up to 1½ hours on the beach either side of low water. Always allow ample time to be within easy reach of the access steps at Bedruthan by the recommended time of two hours after low water. Bedruthan, though, is closed during the winter and, given that the cliffs have a propensity to crumble after stormy weather, it's not advisable to plan a visit to Pentire at that time. Dogs are allowed on both beaches whenever they are open.

If walking from Bedruthan beach it's best to use the National Trust car park (Carnewas), but if tackling the cliffs there's a small National Trust car park at Pentire Farm (Park Head), followed by a walk of around 570yds to the cliff path. There are no facilities here but there's a café, gift shop and toilets at Bedruthan. The nearest bus stop is also at Bedruthan.

The beauty of the area has seen the cliffs and beach feature in the BBC's latest version of Poldark, with scenes shot on nearby Park Head, while episode 1 of season 4 saw Dwight and Caroline meet with Ross and Demelza at Pentire Steps Beach, featuring a lingering shot of Diggory's Island from the clifftop.

There are definitely dangers in visiting Pentire Steps: a vertiginous cliff path, a tide that comes rushing in, and a difficulty of access that is unsuitable for many. However, anyone of reasonable fitness and in possession of a modicum of common sense should take the opportunity to experience the wild grandeur of this magical beach – but keep an eye on the tide and always err on the side of caution.

27. BEDRUTHAN STEPS
SW 848 694
P, PT, DA

Bedruthan Steps is one of the Jewels in the Crown of Cornish beaches, a place of beauty and grandeur that has graced the cover of countless calendars. The coastline here has been eroded over the centuries by the inexorable pounding of the sea, leaving the beach punctuated by towering stacks after the softer rock washed away, and it's these stacks that have made Bedruthan famous.

Viewed from the safety of the cliff at high water it's difficult to believe there could ever be a beach here, such is the power of the sea as it crashes into the stacks and cliff. As the tide ebbs, however, it doesn't take long before the stacks become marooned on an enticing beach of pale golden sand, stretching from Diggory's Island in the north, with Pentire Steps beyond it, to Whitestone Cove in the south, a distance of over half a mile. However, the beach is unique in that a large majority of the thousands who visit every year never set foot on it because, as tempting as it is, many people are unable or unwilling to tackle the daunting 132 steps (depending on the level of the sand) that need to be negotiated in order to reach it, consoling themselves instead with the awe-inspiring view from the clifftop. The steps are steep, winding and uneven, the handrails essential, while the sheer cliffs are stabilised by a metal cage, but the view from the bottom is breathtaking as the height of the stacks becomes apparent; it's like entering a primordial world. A stroll across the flat, firm sand to Pentire Steps is one of the great experiences of a visit to Cornwall, a

63

scramble over the rocks to Whitestone Cove almost as enthralling, but if visiting either extremity its vital to be back within easy reach of the steps no later than two hours after low water as the tide comes in quickly and there's a real danger of being cut off.

It's a beach for exploring rather than the traditional activities: swimming should never be attempted because of powerful rip currents and, while an occasional surfer may be spotted in the sea at the Pentire end, it's suitable only for the experienced. There are unlikely to be any rock pools but there are numerous sand pools, usually around the stacks and smaller outcrops, some of them deep enough for a pleasing paddle. Safety equipment can be found on the steps. The towering cliffs are subject to crumbling, so sitting immediately beneath them isn't recommended, but dogs are allowed on the beach, and it's worth the effort of carefully guiding them down the steps.

Although they don't own the beach, the National Trust own and manage the steps and they deem access to be unsafe during the winter, therefore the beach is officially closed from 1st November until 28th February; anyone spotted on the beach during that time must have used the cliff path at Pentire Steps. Providing access has proved challenging over the years and since the 1960s there have been times when the steps were closed as no safe route was possible. It's these steps that are referred to in the name, rather than the distinctive stacks, the name first being recorded in 1847 when Bedruthan had become a popular outing for Victorian visitors to Newquay; they hired carriages to travel to this rugged coastline, with the local farmer cashing in by providing stalls for the horses on payment of a toll. The Victorians also came up with individual names for the stacks: from the north they are Diggory's Island, Queen Bess Rock, Samaritan Island, Redcove Island, Pendarves Island and Carnewas Island. Queen Bess Rock was so called because of its resemblance to the profile of Elizabeth I; sadly, the relentless pounding of the sea has long since decapitated her. Samaritan Island was named after a ship wrecked on the rock in 1846, resulting in the deaths of 8 of the 11 man crew. A rhyme written at the time suggests the cargo was put to good use:

The Good Samaritan came ashore,
To feed the hungry and clothe the poor,
With barrels of beef and bales of linen,
No poor soul shall want for a shilling.

The Victorians also concocted the legend of a giant called Bedruthan using the beach stacks as stepping stones to cut across the bay. No earlier reference to the story has been found and the likelihood is that it was an early marketing ploy to add some colourful mythology to the landscape. The National Trust-owned cliffs are known as Carnewas and there's a car park there for 190 cars, with a larger seasonal one in a field some 600yds to the north. There is a bus stop at Carnewas. The NT also has a shop and café, as well as toilets, housed in the former count house and buildings of Carnewas Mine, which opened in 1855. It's believed the miners tunnelled into the cliffs from the beach in search of iron, copper and lead, but it can't have been too successful as it was abandoned in 1863, before re-opening five years later and closing for good in 1874. It's possible to spot some adits from the beach, high in the cliff face. In 2014 the Bedruthan and Carnewas area was designated as a Dark Sky Discovery Site because it's classed as one of the best stargazing sites in the UK, an activity that can be enjoyed throughout the year. The same can be said of the view from the cliffs – winter storms seem especially ferocious here - but visiting the beach is only possible between March and October, preferably on a low spring tide. If the prospect of the steps is not too daunting, a walk on Bedruthan is something that has to be experienced.

28. MAWGAN PORTH
SW 848 672
P, PT, RP, SF, SW, L, DA

There's a danger of becoming blasé about the wonderful beaches on this stretch of the Cornish coast but it's impossible not to sing the praises of majestic Mawgan Porth. Lying at the mouth of the beautiful Vale of Lanherne, it's a wide, sandy inlet beach, surrounded by rugged cliffs that rise towards the headlands of Trenance Point to the north and Grange Point and, at low water, Berryl's Point to the south. There's sand at all stages of the tide, although the amount above the high water mark fluctuates, with less after winter storms, while low water sees the tide retreat almost 700yds. At the back of the beach is a small area of dunes, while the shallow River Menalhyl flows from the left-hand corner, splitting the flat, golden sand in two until it disperses towards Grange Point. After Grange Point the beach opens up towards Berryl's Point until at low water it's over 800yds wide, the cliffs pockmarked with caves, but, as the abundance of boulders attest, they are prone to crumbling so care needs to be taken if exploring, and it's not advisable to sit beneath them. It's not great for rock pools but there may be a few at low water in the rocky areas on both sides of the beach. Dogs are allowed all year.

RNLI Lifeguards patrol the beach throughout the summer and swimming should only take place in the areas they designate as safe due to powerful rip currents and the effects of the river, although it is sometimes possible on a rising high tide on a calm day, keeping away from the river. Westerly facing, and so exposed to the

Atlantic swell, it's a busy surfing beach when conditions are right, although not quite as busy as others in the area, which is strange because it's surfable at all stages of the tide, with high and mid-tide best for beginners and *Kingsurf Surf School* on hand to provide lessons. Safety equipment can be found above the beach.

There is easy access directly from the B3276, and another via a path through the dunes, and there's also a path and steps from Trenance on the northern side. There are two good-sized car parks, separated by the river, on the opposite side of the B3276. Toilets can be found nearby, behind the shops and cafés, and the village also has a pub, *The Merrymoor Inn*, across the road from the beach. It's also on a bus route. Best described as functional rather than pretty, the village is almost completely devoted to the tourist industry. Most of the buildings date from after 1920, prior to which the whole area was farmland; when journalist Charles Lewis Hind visited in 1906 he found the only buildings were the coastguard cottages which still stand on the southern cliffs. It's believed to be the cove where, in the 6th century, St Mawgan landed after sailing from Wales or, more likely, Ireland - there were several holy men with similar names. The church and village dedicated to him are about 1½ miles inland. Human activity can certainly be traced back to the 10th century following the discovery in the 1950s of a Dark Age cemetery and three courtyard houses behind what is now a pitch-and-putt golf course.

In 1773 a wealthy Cornish engineer, John Edyvean, attempted to create a canal from Mawgan Porth to Porth, via St Columb, for the transportation of sand and seaweed to be used as fertiliser. A shaft was sunk in the cliffs, on the north side of the beach, so that loads could be drawn up in buckets, and the canal was cut from there to Whitewater, near St Columb. It operated successfully for a while but eventually failed due to faulty construction and Mawgan Porth's unsuitability as a port - there have been at least 10 shipwrecks in the bay. Mr Edyvean lost all of his money and is said to have died of a broken heart shortly after. A remnant of the canal can still be seen on the cliff in the shape of a gorse-filled ditch, while on the beach itself the bottom of the shaft is marked by a trickle of rust-stained water running from the cliff.

There's a very fishy tale associated with Mawgan Porth. In June 1827 a young local man went to investigate a screeching noise coming from a large pool-filled cave but was so terrified by what he saw that he raced back up the beach and could only describe having seen a creature that was 'part human' and had 'long hair hanging about its body'. The next day, three men, probably fishermen, were stood on the cliffs and noticed three creatures sitting together on a rock, just offshore: mermaids! Stranger still, the very next day five more mermaids were spotted and the men who saw them this time claimed to have watched them for more than an hour. They described creatures whose hair was 9 or 10ft long, with some of them basking or sleeping on rocks while others swam in the sea close by. Their upper bodies were coloured 'exactly like that of a Christian', but their arms were 'short and fin-like', their lower parts 'bluish and ending in a tail'. Nowadays the beach is likely to be too busy for mermaids, at least in summer, but visit out of season and it could be that, on a sunny day, the eagle-eyed might just spot one relaxing on an offshore rock. Even if there are no mermaids, though, Mawgan Porth is perfect for all the family and definitely worth exploring.

29. WATERGATE BAY
SW 840 649
P, PT, SF, SW, L, DA

Just a short walk from Mawgan Porth is the equally wonderful, but very different, Watergate Bay, a beach so vast that it's possible to listen to five renditions of Bob Dylan's epic, and very appropriate, masterpiece, *Every Grain of Sand*, while walking from one end to the other. In this case the grains would be light golden in colour and would coalesce to create a beach that at low water stretches for more than 1½ miles from Stem Point in the north to Fruitful Cove in the south. At that time the tide recedes more than 400yds in places, but at high water only a thin strip of sand survives around the main access point, with much of the rest of the beach completely covered. The whole beach is backed by steep, craggy cliffs, up to 200ft high in places, the sand virtually unbroken bar the occasional small rock outcrop, apart from directly beneath the cliffs where the scattered rocks affirm their friable nature. Beware of rock falls, especially if exploring any of the caves that can be found, or any of the rare rock pools - sand pools are far more plentiful. Dogs are allowed all year.

On exceptionally low tides it's possible to walk or scramble over the rocks at the northern end to Stem Cove, just the other side of Stem Point, while, to the south, Fruitful Cove, with its succulently soft sand, is the most sheltered part of the westerly facing beach, which otherwise is very exposed and feels the full force of the Atlantic

69

swell. These extremities are by far the quietest parts of the beach but if visiting them it's essential to be aware of the tide times and allow plenty of time to be back at the main access point before the sea returns. There are a couple of paths up the cliffs at the northern end but they are narrow and very steep and, given the friable nature of the cliffs, cannot be relied upon as a means of escape. To the south the beach is cut off from Whipsiderry by Zacry's Islands, but at low water it's possible to walk around them to the neighbouring beach, the best route being through the small gulley between the cliff face and the rocks. It is, however, exceptionally dangerous once the tide turns as the crossing between the beaches is underwater except for around 2 hours either side of low water. Many people have been rescued between the beaches, so it's absolutely essential to know the tide times if venturing this far as there is no possible escape other than the RNLI Lifeboat. On a brighter note, on low spring tides it's just possible to walk speedily along the sand all the way from Watergate to Newquay Harbour, although it may involve a sprint finish!

There's a 15ft sculpture of a surfer overlooking the beach, made from recycled plastic milk bottles, providing a clue to its popularity as a surfing venue. The surf is consistent at all stages of the tide, and it's one of the few beaches where it's usually better on a high tide. At its best in an easterly wind, Watergate is ideal for both experienced and beginners, and tuition is available from *Extreme Academy*. They also offer lessons in SUP and kite-surfing, the lengthy, often windswept beach being ideal for that activity - *Atlantic Riders* also offer tuition. Watergate is home to the English National Surf Championships and other surfing competitions, and hosts an annual kite-surfing championship. It is also the closest beach to the huge annual Boardmasters festival. RNLI Lifeguards patrol throughout the summer and they operate designated areas for surfing and bathing. Swimming should only take place in the area they declare as safe - strong rip currents make it dangerous at all other times, especially at low water, although it's sometimes possible in calm conditions on a rising high tide, but only with caution and beware of submerged rocks. There is no safety equipment.

Watergate is served by two large car parks, including a seasonal one in a field close to a popular viewing area on the main road, and it's on a bus route. Easy access is provided by steps and a slipway. The beach is owned by the *Watergate Bay Hotel*, which was built in 1900 as a railway terminus hotel for a proposed Newquay to Padstow branch line, but the railway was never built. During WW2 it became an RAF Officers Mess, but fell into disrepair during the 1960s until it was converted back to a hotel in the 1970s. At that time there was just a small, traditional beach shop here, but gradually the whole area has been transformed, especially after the shop made way for Jamie Oliver's *Fifteen* restaurant in 2006. Then the *Extreme Sports Academy*, providing exhilarating water sports opportunities for adrenalin junkies, really took off and soon the whole area was redeveloped with expensive apartments and holiday homes built within the footprint of the hotel land, while across the road some shabby older buildings were demolished to make way for apartments. With restaurants, cafés, and a shop, plus toilets across the road on Tregurrian Hill, there is everything the modern tourist needs.

Tregurrian is an alternative name for the beach, a derivation of *Porth Tregoryan*, 'Cove at Coryan's Farm'. The present name is a bit of a mystery but it has no Nixonian connotations, having been in use since 1813. Every year or so there's a spectacular *Polo on the Beach* event held here. In 1967 The Beatles shot a scene for their *Magical Mystery Tour* film here, although it failed to make the final cut. The 2008 TV series *Echo Beach* and the 1999 film *The Magical Legends of the Leprechauns,* starring Randy Quaid and Orla Brady were filmed here, as were scenes from the 1953 film *The Master of Ballantrae*, starring Errol Flynn, all of them taking advantage of a wild, unspoilt beach, big enough to cope comfortably with the crowds who flock here during the summer. It brings delight to families, adrenaline junkies, and those seeking a bit of solitude on a beach of broad, open spaces, high cliffs, and huge breaking waves. Delightful!

30. WHIPSIDERRY BEACH
SW 830 631
P, PT, RP, SW, DA

Separated from Watergate Bay by Zacry's Islands, Whipsiderry is one of the lesser known beaches on the north coast, unjustly overshadowed by its neighbours, the endless sands of Watergate, the popular Porth, and the Newquay town beaches. This lack of fame can only be because it's a tidal beach, completely covered at high water, and not visible from the road or even from the Coast Path, only coming into view from the very edge of the cliff. In addition, access is only possible for those of reasonable fitness with 135 steep and uneven steps needing to be negotiated, although there is the bonus of a smugglers' hole or mining adit to look out for in the cliffs. The nearest car park is in Porth, from where there's a very steep, 400yd uphill walk, which is not conducive to persuading visitors to forsake the delights of Porth, and even many of the more inquisitive settle for a walk along Trevelgue Head, from where they can see Whipsiderry, but not visit. There is a little roadside parking available at the top of the hill, but room only for a maximum of five cars; the bus also stops there. It is possible to walk along the shore from both the neighbouring beaches at low water, but only when tide times have been checked as there's a real threat of being cut off from mid-tide onwards: there is a genuine danger of misjudging the tide by thinking there's plenty of time to walk to or from Watergate Bay – there is, provided the tide is still ebbing!

The name derives from the old mining terms, *Whips,* a name for marker flags, and *Derrick,* a lifting device situated over a shaft. There is plenty evidence of mine workings, notably in the enormous island in the middle of the cove, known variously as Black Humphry's Rock, Flory's Island, or Flag Island, while some of the boulders scattered across the beach contain iron ore. Black Humphry was a smuggler who used to hide on the island, which was once even bigger than it is today. The tide retreats over 300yds to reveal a glorious beach of flat golden sand, with a small patch of stones near the access point. From an apparently narrow cove at high water it expands to a remarkable width of 800yds at low, stretching from Zacry's Islands to Porth Island, also known as Trevelgue Head, and from there it's possible to reach Porth Beach, although there are some very slippery and large rocks to negotiate and it may involve a bit of paddling. The perforated rock guarding the gap between the island and the mainland is known as Norwegian Rock.

Backed by high, undulating cliffs, Whipsiderry has a wonderfully wild feel, and there are numerous caves and arches to explore, with many of the caves bequeathed imaginative names by the ever-helpful Victorians. The most notable is known as The Cathedral Cavern, and contains a large pillar, a pool of water and several intersecting tunnels; white marble was quarried here in the past, with drill holes in the walls and a shaft to the cliff top still visible. There are also two fine, smaller caves named according to their contents: Fern Cavern and Boulder Cavern. One of the most famous caves was the 200ft long and 60ft wide Banqueting Hall or Concert Cavern, so called because, at one time, a piano was wheeled in at low tide for candlelight concerts! Sadly, it was blown up in 1987 for safety reasons. There are usually some large rock pools to explore amongst the outcrops, while many of the rocks are festooned with mussels. Strong rip currents make swimming dangerous at low water but it is possible with care on calm days on a rising high tide. There can be good surfing, but it's not as popular as other beaches in the area. Safety equipment can be found by the access steps. Dogs are allowed all year. There are no facilities, the nearest being in Porth. Be aware that the cliffs are prone to crumbling, which makes sitting at the back of the beach inadvisable, and as the tide comes in quickly it's important to be close to the access steps in good time. The difficult access will rule Whipsiderry out for some people, but anyone sufficiently fit should certainly pay a visit, when it won't take long to understand why those troublesome steps have been referred to as a *Stairway to Heaven* – this is definitely Beach Heaven!

31. PORTH
SW 831 628
P, PT, SF, SW, RP, L, DR

The village of Porth may still proclaim its independence but in reality it has long since been swallowed up by the urban sprawl of Newquay, although that should not deter anyone from visiting this magnificent beach. It's an inlet beach, but one where there is plenty of sand above the high water mark, usually being more than 100yds deep and 300yds wide in the summer. This can change depending on weather conditions, and winter storms have led to surges that not only engulfed the end of the beach, but swept right across the road. The tide retreats beyond the mouth of the inlet, a distance of 900yds, while the mouth narrows to a width of under 200yds, thus creating a long, almost boot-shaped beach. The gradient is very shallow, so the tide comes in quickly, while the surrounding headlands rise up on each side to provide plenty of shelter from any Atlantic breezes, with the southern side more sheltered, especially the tiny inlet mysteriously called the 'Great Cupboard'. The river running along the right-hand side of the beach can be surprisingly deep and fast-flowing and forms a barrier to the more secluded areas on that side, but it's usually easy enough to paddle across and provides much pleasure for children.

At low water there's an easy walk around the southern headland to the sheltered Wine Cove and from there to Lusty Glaze Beach, while on the northern side it's possible to clamber over the rocks and under the footbridge that links to Porth Island to reach Whipsiderry, but be prepared for a bit of paddling as well. On some low tides it's possible to walk around the island to the craggy inlet of Long Cove, the most secluded part of the beach, but if visiting any of these extremities it's vital to be aware of the tide to avoid being cut off. There are some beautiful and deep rock pools dotted around the island, plus a few others on the southern side. Dog restrictions apply throughout the summer.

Among the excellent facilities available are a shop, a seasonal refreshments van, toilets, and a pub, the *Mermaid Inn*, which is actually on the beach itself. In the winter of 2018 the inn's outdoor seating area was covered by a 5ft sand drift; the bay acts as a wind tunnel that results in sand building up at the top of the beach and on the road by the inn. Car parking is allowed on a corner of the beach, off Porth Beach Road, large enough for 60 cars but it is tide dependant, while there's a much larger car park off Alexandra Road. There's a bus stop at the back of the beach, and there is easy, level access. Swimming is fine on an incoming tide but strong currents around the mouth of the inlet make it unsafe at low water. It's also important not to swim anywhere near to the river at any stage of the tide, while swimming on an ebbing tide should only be undertaken if the RNLI Lifeguards designate a safe area. On a calm day it's possible to paddle and wade out a long way due to the shallow gradient of the beach. Exposure to Atlantic swells makes it a great location for surfing, although be aware that it is not permitted during the summer season while the lifeguards are on duty, due to overcrowding. Surf is best at high water, and it is suitable for all levels, with the *Blue Surf School* providing lessons. Safety equipment can be found by the Lifeguard Hut and at the back of the beach.

Porth used to be called St Columb Porth and was once a small shipbuilding port where coal was imported from South Wales. Nowadays it forms the northern limit of Newquay, with a few tentacles snaking out to Whipsiderry. On the north side of the beach is Porth Island, also known as Trevelgue Head, which offers an attractive and, in a brisk wind, bracing walk around its perimeter, with panoramic views of Newquay and the north coast to enjoy. It's connected to the mainland by a short footbridge and even has its own blowhole, best seen at mid-tide when there is a swell. The island has been occupied since the Mesolithic period but most of the remains unearthed by archaeologists date from the Iron Age, including round houses and the ramparts of a cliff castle. On the southern side of the beach is the *Glendorgal Hotel*, built in 1850, which was for many years the home of the Tangye family, including Derek, the author of the *Minack Chronicles*. In 1950 the house was opened as a hotel by his brother, Nigel Tangye. In September 1967 Paul McCartney was filmed riding a tandem on the beach for the film *Magical Mystery Tour*.

32. NEWQUAY - LUSTY GLAZE
SW 824 624
P, PT, RP, SF, SW, L, DR

The second of the Newquay Bay beaches, and the first official Newquay town beach, is the mysteriously named Lusty Glaze, which shares many of the characteristics of its neighbouring town beaches, Tolcarne, Great Western and Towan: flat, sandy, and shielded from the majority of strong currents and winds by the natural lee of Towan Head. They lie below sheer cliffs that have been battered into jagged hollows by the unrelenting and implacable sea, while the town of Newquay, loved and loathed in equal measure, sprawls on a broad plateau above.

 Newquay has always divided opinion. As far back as 1907 the journalist C Lewis Hind suggested that people arriving in the town "must be prepared for disillusionment....the railway, the jerry builder, the heedlessness of those in authority who allowed the town to grow without artistic direction, have between them spoilt a site that might have been one of the finest watering places in the kingdom." In 1910 Arthur L. Salmon stated bluntly that "Modern Newquay seems to have striven to render itself uninteresting." Even worse, in the 1990s and 2000s the town became synonymous with stag and hen parties and the alcohol-fuelled antics of teenagers on their first holidays without parents. The main street was lined with clubs, pubs and amusement arcades but, eventually, the local community had enough of the rowdy behaviour and demanded change. Recent years have seen a concerted effort to broaden the town's appeal with the opening of boutique hotels, trendy bistros, cafés and bakeries, and it succeeded to such an extent that the town was voted best family holiday destination by readers of Coast magazine, and remains the UK's premier surfing destination and one of the leading seaside resorts in the country. Despite these improvements there are those who claim that although Newquay is in Cornwall there is very little of Cornwall in it, but this is far from true: dig beneath the tourist town surface and a fascinating, and very Cornish, history emerges.

 That Cornish heritage is nowhere more apparent than at Lusty Glaze. Near the back of the cove are the remains of an inclined plane intended to haul boats from the beach up to the southern section of Edyvean's Canal, built in 1773, which we encountered at Mawgan Porth. Unfortunately, the sandy soil was unable to hold water so this section of the canal was never used, while the incline was badly damaged by a landslide in 2014. It's one of the few coastal beaches to have been rich in iron ore, and on the north-eastern side is a 200ft deep cave that still bears the scars of the mining that took place here. At low water the ore was carried from the beach to the harbour by horse and cart, but at other stages of the tide it was transported by small blue boats, giving credence to the translation of the name as 'a place to view blue boats' from the Cornish *Listri*, 'boats' and *glas*, 'blue, green'. It's not known whether the mine ran dry or if it simply became financially unviable but in the 1920s the beach was transformed into a 'glamorous ladies and gentlemen's bathing beach' featuring brightly coloured beach huts, donkey rides and even butlers! While there aren't any butlers or donkey rides now, Lusty Glaze retains enough quirky charm to be popular with both visitors and the local community; there are still beach huts available for hire, plus a bar and restaurant, and the *Lusty Glaze Adventure Centre*, which offers activities in the water, on the beach and on the cliffs, including tight-rope walking. In addition to all this breathless activity, Lusty Glaze has become a favourite location for bespoke weddings, and there are free live music evenings every week of the year - Wednesday in summer, Friday in winter – with the beach transformed into a spectacular concert venue for its *Sundowner Sessions*.

Throughout its evolution from a working beach to a genteel Edwardian resort to today's vibrant cove, one thing has remained constant: the beauty of the beach. There's sand at all stages of the tide, around 45yds deep and 100yds wide at high water, surrounded by high cliffs that form a horseshoe shaped amphitheatre. At low water it expands way beyond the headlands to some 400yds in depth, making it possible to walk around to the secluded Wine Cove in the east, and sometimes onto Porth Beach, while westwards is another secluded area known as 'Criggars', with Tolcarne Beach and the rest of Newquay Bay easily accessible beyond. There are several caves and sheltered gullies on both sides, and there may be an occasional rock pool, but be aware that these areas are cut off from the main beach by the returning tide, so it's important to check the tide times and keep an eye on the incoming sea. All the cliffs of Newquay Bay are prone to crumbling and in March 2018 a landslide at Lusty Glaze caused damage to some of the beach huts, which at that time of the year are used for storage: look out for warning notices and keep away from those areas. Dog restrictions apply during the summer. Public toilets are situated near to the beach huts. There is a car park on the cliffs above the beach, with a walk down 133 steep and irregular steps to follow, making access impossible for wheelchairs and prams.

Swimming at Lusty Glaze is best undertaken when RNLI Lifeguards are present during the summer. It's a popular surfing beach, suitable for all levels, with experienced surfers tending to prefer 'Criggars' and Wine Cove. As a general rule, the further north-east along the bay the more exposed the beaches become as the amount of shelter provided by Towan Head reduces, so Lusty Glaze is slightly less suitable for beginners than Towan Beach. There are also rocky outcrops to be wary of as they are difficult to spot at high water. *Lusty Glaze Adventure Centre* offer tuition for beginners. Safety equipment can be found at the back of the beach.

Like much of Newquay, the privately owned Lusty Glaze has benefited from healthy investment in recent years, to the extent that it was crowned Beach of the Year in 2017 by the Sunday Times. It can be whatever you want it to be: an adrenaline filled adventure playground, a sun worshipper's haven, somewhere to relax over a good meal or even the ideal spot for a romantic beach wedding; and for anyone wanting to savour a classically wild Cornish beach, the rugged cliffs, rocky gullies, sand, surf and sea are still there, but best enjoyed when the summer crowds have disappeared.

33. NEWQUAY - TOLCARNE BEACH
SW 817 619
P, PT, RP, SF, SW, L, DR

Nestled between Lusty Glaze and Great Western, Tolcarne is the largest of the four beaches that join up at low water to create the mile of soft golden sand that makes Newquay such a family favourite. Like its neighbours, it's encompassed by high, dramatic cliffs, with access provided by over 130 steep, narrow steps and an equally steep winding road, which is not open to traffic and probably too steep for wheelchairs or prams. A small landslip early in 2017 resulted in the road being temporarily closed off to the public. The back of the beach is dominated by *Tolcarne Beach Village*, virtually a self-contained mini-resort with a bar and restaurant, an organic café and a beach shop, and accommodation in houses, cabins and apartments. Windbreaks, loungers, surfboards and wetsuits can be hired. There's even a cold water shower that's ideal for washing down surfboards and wetsuits or rinsing sandy feet. Toilets can be found towards the west side and on the access road.

There is plenty of sand at all stages of the tide: even when the tide is in it's around 200yds long and perhaps 30yds deep, while at low water it stretches way beyond the cliffs to perhaps 350yds deep and 490yds wide until it merges with Great Western and the 'Criggars' part of Lusty Glaze. There are a number of caves and drainage adits in the cliffs, the latter the only surviving evidence of the extensive mining that occurred here in the 1860s. There are usually a few rock pools on the fringes of the beach, which is cleaned twice daily during the summer, when dog restrictions also apply. The nearest car park is behind the *Hotel Bristol,* across the road from the beach.

As with all the beaches in the bay it's best to swim when the RNLI Lifeguards are present, keeping to the designated bathing area. The waves here are frequently described as 'mellow', making it suitable for all levels of surfers, although at high water the infamous 'Tolcarne Wedge' can change that if the conditions are favourable. Caused by waves refracting off the cliffs and running perpendicular to the shore, the wedge is a favourite of expert bodyboarders and it can be extremely busy when in full flow. The *Surf and Adventure Centre* based on the beach offer tuition for surfers.

There are fine views of Tolcarne from the Barrowfields, a grassy open space on the cliff that was once the site of 17 Bronze Age burial mounds, but only three remain after the rest were destroyed by a local farmer in 1821. Excavations revealed charred cooking pots and a coarse pottery burial urn containing the remains of a chieftain who lived here some 3,500 years ago. A local legend describes this as a haunted place: in the dead of night when the moon is new and the mist rolls off the sea, the ominous sound of galloping horses can be heard overhead, foreshadowing their arrival seconds later, several yards in the air and ridden by a headless horseman. The beach name comes from the Cornish *tal karn,* 'next to rock-pile or crag' or 'holed crag', possibly a reference to the Barrowfields.

Purists might quibble with all the developments but there's no doubt that Tolcarne is another beautiful Newquay beach. It tends to be slightly less busy than the other beaches in the bay but is still best visited out of season.

34. NEWQUAY - GREAT WESTERN BEACH
SW 815 618
P, PT, RP, SF, SW, L, DA

The third of Newquay's beaches derives its name from the Great Western Railway, whose Atlantic Coast Line brought passengers here from 1877, leading to the town's development as a tourist centre. The line was the brainchild of industrialist J T Treffry in 1849 as a link to the harbour from his mines in the Newlyn East area and his china clay pits around St Dennis. Loads were brought to the railway station by steam engine and then pulled along a tramway by horses, before being lowered to the harbour via a steeply inclined tunnel. The last loads of coal and china clay were handled in 1921 and the tram track, the route of which can be followed from between a *Travelodge* and the *Griffin Inn*, was used for the last time in 1931. Prior to the arrival of the railway the beach was called Bothwick's Beach.

Situated close to the town centre, Great Western is a popular beach but tends to be less busy than Towan. Backed by sheer, high cliffs, it consists of several small coves, including Killacourt Cove to the west, that offer a degree of seclusion during the busy summer season, while the cliffs contain some splendid caves and old mining adits. Be aware, though, that as with the other beaches in the bay, the cliffs are prone to crumbling. At high water there is only a thin strip of sand, just under 100yds long and perhaps 25yds deep in the summer, less in winter. Low water sees the emergence of an alluring spread of pale golden sand, some 340yds wide and 350yds deep, broken only by a few rock outcrops, mainly near to the cliffs, where there may be an occasional rock pool. One of the outcrops bears the nickname of Bishop's Rock due to its resemblance to a bishop's mitre. In May 2018 Great Western became the first Newquay beach to be awarded a prestigious Blue Flag and please note that although well behaved dogs are allowed all year they are not allowed in the blue flag area, running from the access point to Tolcarne, between May and September.

Access is via a steep, winding road to the left of the *Great Western Hotel*, with a slipway leading down to the sand. For those unable or unwilling to venture all the way down there's a viewing area with seats just before the steepest part of the descent. The nearest car park is by the railway station – no cars are allowed on the access road, which had to be closed on a couple of occasions in recent years due to landslips. The hotel owes its existence to the railway company, and of a similar vintage, at the other end of the beach, is the *Hotel Victoria*, which once had lift access directly on to Killacourt Cove. Unfortunately, this unique route to the beach was closed several years ago on safety grounds, but the steps and tunnel can still be seen. Both these buildings have an elegantly regal appearance but the same can't be said of the huge block of the former Barracuda nightclub that looms over the central part of the beach, looking like the back end of an inner city warehouse: with all the developments there've been in Newquay it's a shame that no-one has seen fit to demolish this eyesore.

At the bottom of the access road are some utilitarian buildings that have been enhanced in recent years to include *The Slope Beach Bar + Kitchen,* serving refreshments including a delicious 'gourmet burger', and the *NQY Surf School* for lessons and equipment hire. In addition there is *Sandbox,* set up in a converted shipping container for ice creams, pasties and other refreshments. Seasonal public toilets are also situated here.

RNLI Lifeguards patrol the beach throughout the summer and it's best to swim only when they are present. It's believed to have been the UK's original surfing beach, with the waves being ridden by the lifeguards of the early 1960s, and it remains a popular spot, the moderate-sized waves being fine for novices. Safety equipment can be found by the surf school.

Great Western is another fine Newquay beach, perfect for all the family but, as with the other beaches in the bay, the best time to visit is at low water when it's possible to enjoy the wonderful walk to the adjoining beaches.

35. NEWQUAY - TOWAN BEACH
SW 809 617
P, PT, RP, SF, SW, L, DA

Towan Beach is close enough to the centre of Newquay to sometimes be mistakenly called Town Beach and, consequently, it's the most crowded, certainly in the summer, being popular with families, dog walkers, surfers, and just about everyone else! *Towan* is Cornish for sand dunes, which is odd for a beach with no dunes, but it's actually a remnant of Newquay's original name, *Towan Blistra,* or, as it was first recorded in 1308, *Tewynplustri,* and refers to the dunes found at the back of Fistral, with the meaning of the second half of the name unclear.

At low water there's about 350yds of flat, golden sand flanked by the harbour wall on one side and merging with Great Western Beach on the other, and it's usually more sheltered than the other beaches in the bay, with the bulk of Towan Head providing protection from the prevailing winds. There's an area of rock outcrops near the harbour wall with numerous rock pools to explore, plus three caves. A 6ft high tunnel runs through the harbour wall but it's usually buried under the sand except for the top arch stones. The main feature of the beach and the star of a thousand postcards is the huge rock outcrop known as The Island, which it appears to be when the tide is in, but is surrounded by sand and smaller outcrops at low water. It's joined to the mainland by a graceful suspension bridge, constructed in 1902. The house perched on top was built in 1910 and was once home to the famous scientist Sir Oliver Lodge. Sir Arthur Conan Doyle, author of Sherlock Holmes and a fellow spiritualist, attended séances held on the Island. Since then it's been a tearoom, an art gallery, and is now a luxury holiday let after the previous owners, Lord and Lady Long, left in 2012, having had enough of the late night bedlam created by partygoers on the beach. Prior to the creation of the suspension bridge it's believed that chickens were kept on the Island and it was also used as a potato patch. Around that time religious services for children were held there on Sunday afternoons, the children climbing to the top via curving pathways cut into the rock face. At the foot of the Island is a natural bathing pool that has fallen into disrepair and is often filled with sand, but there is a campaign to restore it to its former glory.

Backed by a sea wall and promenade, access to the sand is via by a slipway and two short flights of steps. Dogs are allowed on the beach all year. At high water it's completely covered, and it's then that the promenade and the grassy expanse on the clifftop, known as Killacourt, come into their own, with plenty of seats provided from which to enjoy the view. The promenade was once home to a fish cellar, a mineral water factory, a steam laundry and public baths but it exemplifies Newquay's attempts to shake off its downmarket party image: revamped and refreshed in recent years, it's now home to a bakery, fish and chip shop and other local fresh food sellers, while deckchairs and windbreaks can be hired. A limited number of beach huts are available for hire and it's also the home of *Newquay Activity Centre,* which offers courses in surfing, SUP, kayaks, and coasteering. The most prominent building, though, houses the *Blue Reef Aquarium*, which is well worth a visit, even on a sunny day. Sand chairs can be hired, and toilets are also situated in the Aquarium. The nearest car park is on Fore Street with a walk down the steep Beach Road to follow. Alternatively, there are steps from the green and pleasant Killacourt to the promenade, and another flight of steps from the rocky corner of the beach to the harbour.

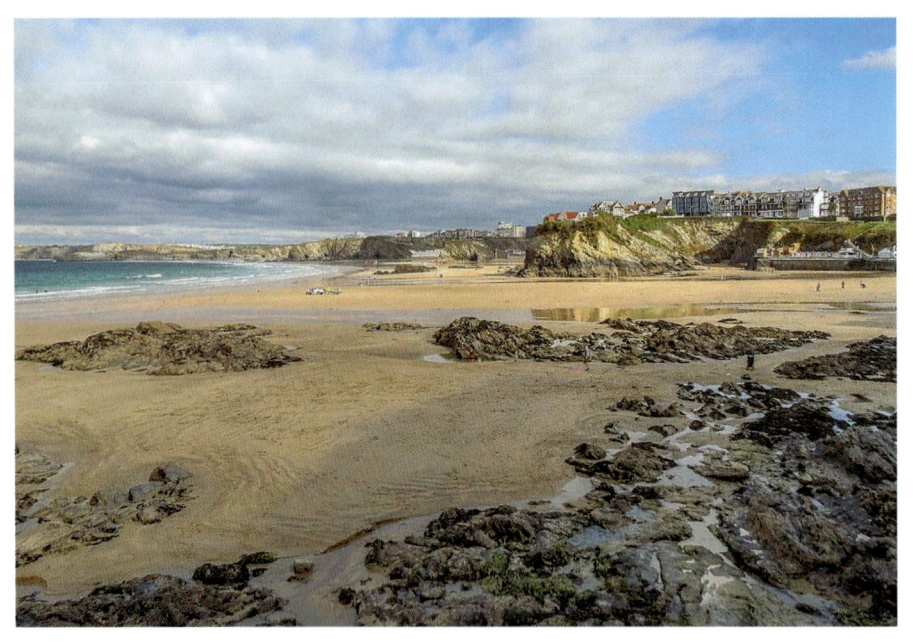

The shelter provided by Towan Head means that the beach avoids the worst of the Atlantic swell and big waves but, even so, safety can only be guaranteed by following the instructions of RNLI Lifeguards who patrol throughout the summer. The absence of big waves makes it suitable for surfers of any level, and it's the best spot in the bay for beginners - *Escape Surf School* offer lessons from the beach. Under a local bye-law, surfing at Towan is not permitted at high water and it isn't feasible for a couple of hours afterwards. It is surfable all year and for that reason is very popular during the winter. Safety equipment can be found above the beach, as can a first aid post during the summer.

The combination of beauty, history and location in the heart of Newquay makes Towan as fine a 'town beach' as it's possible to be. Yes, it can be unbearably busy during the summer but a visit out of season, or early on a summer morning when the tide is out and it's possible to follow the sand all the way to Lusty Glaze, is an experience that shouldn't be missed.

36. NEWQUAY HARBOUR
SW 807 620
P, PT, SW, DA

The final and most unheralded beach of Newquay Bay is the Harbour Beach, cut off from its neighbours by the South Quay but possessing what is reputed to be the softest sand in the town. The first record of a harbour here was in 1439 when permission was given for 'the construction and maintenance of a *keye* on the seashore at *Tewen Blustry*', a variation of the original name of what was then a small fishing village. By 1602 the village was being referred to as *New Keye*, the origin of the modern name, but it wasn't until the mid-19th century, when industrialist J T Treffry decided he needed a port on the north coast to serve his mines and china clay works, that the harbour prospered, with most of what we see today being built in that period. 1841 saw a new north quay built and in 1872, when the harbour was at its busiest, an isolated stone pier was constructed to expand capacity, connected to South Quay by a 150ft long timber trestle. Loads were brought to the harbour via a steeply inclined tunnel and tram tracks were laid along South Quay and onto the centre pier, enabling more iron ore, processed fish, china clay and stone to be loaded onto the waiting cargo vessels. At the same time the pilchard fishing industry had expanded, reaching its peak during the 1860s when there were 12 fishing seines. These were boom years and town's population expanded dramatically, but as the century drew to a close the port was in decline as Cornwall's mining and pilchard industries collapsed and the harbour was deemed to be too small to cope with the new steam powered ships. The last vessel to bring cargo and leave fully laden was the schooner, *Hetty*, in 1921. Luckily, as we saw at Great Western, the arrival of the railway in 1877 saw the beginnings of Newquay's reincarnation as a holiday resort, but the harbour's days as the fulcrum of activity were numbered: from now on it was the town's beaches and dramatic coastline that would be the centre of attention.

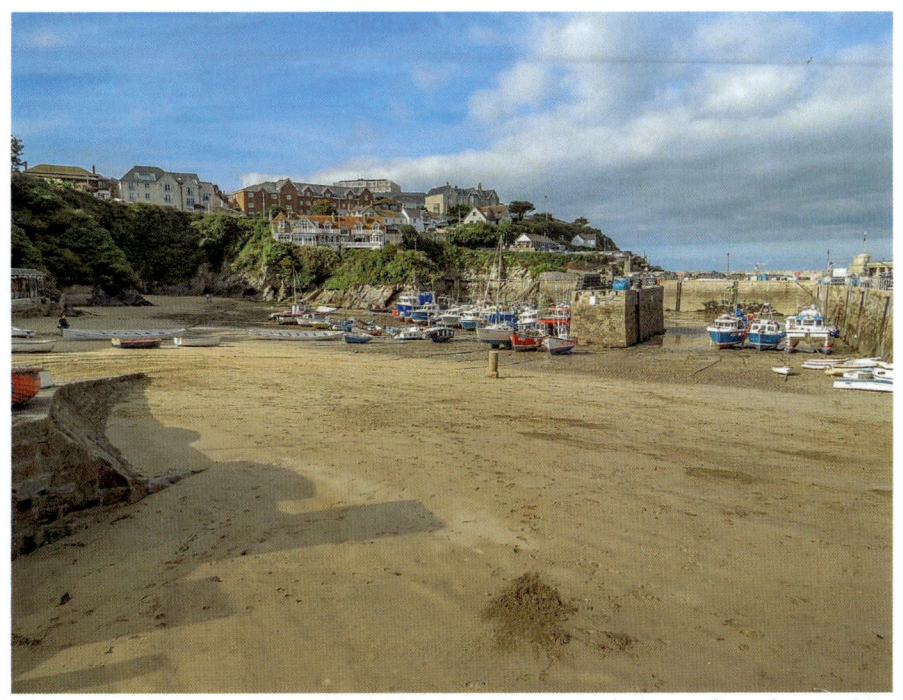

Today, the harbour is still used as a place of work, with the beach often crammed with a fishing fleet of brightly coloured boats and leisure craft, and collections of lobster pots and crates stacked along the pier arms. The RNLI boathouse, gig clubhouse, seaman's mission, restaurant and other fishing and diving related businesses populate the quaysides. The Lifeboat House was built on the site of the former Seaman's Mission, beside which was one of Newquay's many wells, once used to supply schooners with fresh water. The Mission began as a 'Book Bag Mission' in 1883, when Christian books and tracts and other 'improving' books were taken to ships for the crews to read when off duty. In 1891 a wooden chapel and library was opened and a missionary employed, allowing a service to be held on Sundays for the fishermen and seamen. Following the building of the new lifeboat house in 1994 the Mission reopened in a new building just a few feet away from where the old wooden chapel had stood, and it continues to be used by fishermen, holiday makers and locals alike. The steep tunnel built by Treffry is still there, housing the rowing club's gigs. Gigs were used in the 19th century to ferry pilots out to ships, to enable them to be guided safely into the harbour; in 1840 there were four such gigs working out of the harbour and three of them, *Treffry*, built in 1838, *Dove* (1820) and *Newquay* (1812) are still in recreational use today.

The harbour is best reached by walking down the fairly steep South Quay Hill, off Fore Street, with a wide, if uneven, slipway leading down to the beach. It's linked to Towan Beach by a flight of steps, and there are also steps down from North Quay, accessible at low water. The character of the harbour changes with the ebb and flow of the tide, with just a strip of sand next to the slipway at high water, plus a few small, isolated coves that become accessible as the tide recedes, until, at low water, the whole harbour dries out, leaving the brightly coloured boats stranded and allowing access between the south and north quays, although there may well be various ropes and chains to negotiate. On extreme low tides it's possible to walk around South Quay to Towan Beach. It's a very sheltered spot, from both the wind and the exuberant clamour of the town; there's a sense of isolation despite the overlooking buildings, while the rubble revetment wall is topped by verdant cliffs that are emblazoned with colourful flowers during the summer. It's not noted for rock pools but keep an eye out for the grey seals that have made the harbour their home, spending their days basking in the sun and cadging food from returning boats. At high water it's a popular fishing spot for anglers. Dogs are allowed on the beach all year. With no problem from any currents it is safe for swimming at high water but be aware that it's very busy with both working and leisure boats, with fishing and scenic trips available from the harbour. Safety equipment can be found at various points on the quayside. *Newquay Water Sports Centre* is based in Treffry's tunnel, offering a huge range of water sports and land based activities, and often using the sheltered harbour water for lessons. It's not suitable for surfing. *The Boathouse Restaurant* below the cliffs sits on the site of an old boatbuilding yard, and there's usually an ice cream van present during the summer, with plenty of other places for refreshments found in the surrounding streets. There are toilets on South Quay.

Those who think Newquay is all parties and surfing would do well to visit its harbour, one of the most beautiful in Cornwall and steeped in Cornish history, and those searching for a relaxing contrast to the often hectic activity of the other beaches should certainly seek it out. In a way it's a shame that a proposal to open up Treffry's tunnel as a means of access never came to fruition as that would have enabled visitors to travel more easily between the town and the harbour. There are days, though, when the harbour is exceptionally busy, with a Lifeboat Day and a Harbour Day being held every August, while September sees the quays crammed with kiosks during *Newquay Food Festival*, but usually it remains a place of refuge with enough activity to entertain and a beach that is the most underrated in the town.

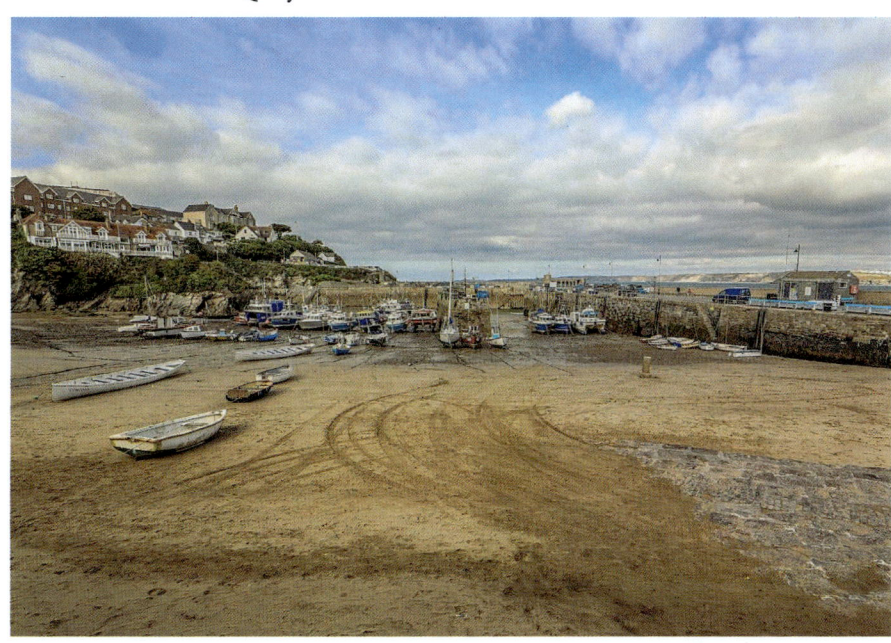

37. NEWQUAY - LITTLE FISTRAL and NUN COVE
SW 800 627
P, PT, RP, SF, DA

Little Fistral lies on the exposed western side of Towan Head and so feels the full force of the Atlantic waves which, over millennia, have shaped and scoured the low cliff into numerous gullies and coves, including, just to the south, Nun Cove. It's another underrated Newquay beach, usually ignored by the thousands that flock to its much bigger and more famous neighbour, making it the ideal beach for those who want to escape the crowds but still enjoy the sight of giant waves rolling into the bay. There's no beach at high water but the ebbing tide reveals a strip of surprisingly gritty sand, followed by a band of wave cut rock platforms, home to plenty of rock pools. More sand emerges at low water, at which time the beach is linked to the usually boisterously busy Fistral, allowing more visitors. Nun Cove sits between the two and is effectively just a continuation of Little Fistral. Nuns are tiny, flesh-coloured cowry shells which the eagle-eyed might be able to spot in the little pools and hollows left by the backwash from waves.

The beach lies below the 'neck' of the imposing Towan Head where the cliffs are lower and eroded and pockmarked with small hollows and caves known as the Pisky Holes; local folklore suggests that they were once, and perhaps still are, home to some of Cornwall's diminutive fairy folk. In 1989, toe-bones of an extinct Giant Elk were found in the cliff face, about 6ft above the beach, showing how much higher the sand level was when

88

the animal was living about 75,000 years ago. At low water it's possible to spot some large rounded boulders which were part of an ambitious scheme devised by J T Treffry who, following the success of his first harbour, proposed a second be built on the west side of Towan Head. Known as 'The Harbour of Refuge' it would have been accessible at all stages of the tide and linked to the other by a canal cut through the neck of the headland. Building began in 1848 with the construction of a granite breakwater but following Treffry's death in 1850 the project was abandoned.

Towan Head car park is directly above the beach, with a set of metal steps leading to a fairly steep slope down to the beach. It's also possible to scramble down the cliff at a couple of other points. Next to the car park is Newquay's Old Lifeboat House, with its slipway on the other side of the headland reputed to have the steepest gradient in Britain. The station closed in 1934 and later became an artist's studio. Public toilets can be found at the headland end of the car park, and there is usually an ice cream van parked there in the summer. Dogs are allowed on the beach all year.

The RNLI Lifeguards who patrol Fistral keep an eye on Little Fistral but don't encourage swimming due to rip currents and strong undertow on what is a steeply-shelving beach. Surfing is best at low water but the large waves here mean that it's best left to the experienced, with everyone else advised to keep to Fistral. Just to the north of the beach are Cribbar Rocks, which, when conditions are right, produce a legendary wave, known as 'The Cribbar', some 25ft high. It's a popular beach for kite-surfing out of season or early in the morning. There's safety equipment by the steps that lead to the beach.

Although forever destined to remain in the shadow of its big brother, Little Fistral provides spectacular views of Fistral, Pentire Point East and 'The Goose' islet off Crantock; and with the possibility of spotting seals or dolphins frolicking in the sea and for a ringside view of some of the best surfers in the world in action, it's a beach that is well worth visiting.

38. NEWQUAY - FISTRAL BEACH
SW 800 622
P, PT, RP, SF, SW, L, DA

Arguably the most famous beach in Cornwall and the capital of UK surfing, the magnificent Fistral is a linear beach of more than 900yds in length and, at low water, a depth of over 400yds, at which time it stretches from Little Fistral in the north to the tiny Great and Little Toddy Coves in the south. There's sand at all stages of the tide, with just a thin strip at high, but the ebbing tide unveils a vast expanse of pale sand with rocky areas at both ends that contain rock pools, and provide a bit of shelter and seclusion from the crowds that flock here during the summer. Behind the beach is a steep sand dune system, the majority of which now forms the links for *Newquay Golf Club*.

Neatly divided into two, North and South Fistral, the beach is a favourite of families as well as surfers with South being the quieter end, while the surfers generally favour North. There are numerous easy access points with the main one being a gentle slope from the car park in the north, suitable for wheelchairs and prams, while South can be reached by steps from Esplanade Road, where there is some roadside parking. In addition, there's a path across the golf course to the centre of the beach from Tower Road car park. Dogs are allowed all year. There are toilets at both ends and one café at South Fistral, while North has cafés, bars, restaurants and shops situated in the *International Surf Centre*, plus a surf school and equipment hire.

That complex was built in 2003 to capitalise, or enhance, Fistral's growing fame as a surfing venue. What makes Fistral so special? Its north-westerly orientation exposes it to the full force of the Atlantic swell and the virtually straight beach is enclosed by two headlands, Towan Head and Pentire Point East, which funnel in powerful, hollow waves. On any beach the quality of waves is dependent on the sand banks and Fistral's are perfect for producing unpredictable and challenging waves that regularly reach heights of between 6 and 8ft, unlike, for instance, Towan where the banks are flatter, producing waves that are straight, predictable, and more suitable for beginners. Fistral is also unusual in that it can be surfed at all stages of the tide, with the waves produced at low water very different to those found at high. Unsurprisingly, then, it regularly hosts national and international competitions, notably the annual *Boardmasters Festival*. For those keen to learn or hone their skills there are two surf schools, *Quiksilver*, and *Fistral Beach Surf School*.

The heavy swell that makes the beach suitable for surfing makes it unsuitable for swimming, apart from on exceptionally calm days. Even then it's best to swim only when RNLI Lifeguards are present and deem it safe: North Fistral is patrolled from Easter until the end of October, and South during July and August only. Safety equipment can be found at both ends of the beach. Incidentally, 'Fistral' probably derives from *Porth an Bystel*, 'cove of foul water', a reference to the huge waves that make it an unsuitable landing site.

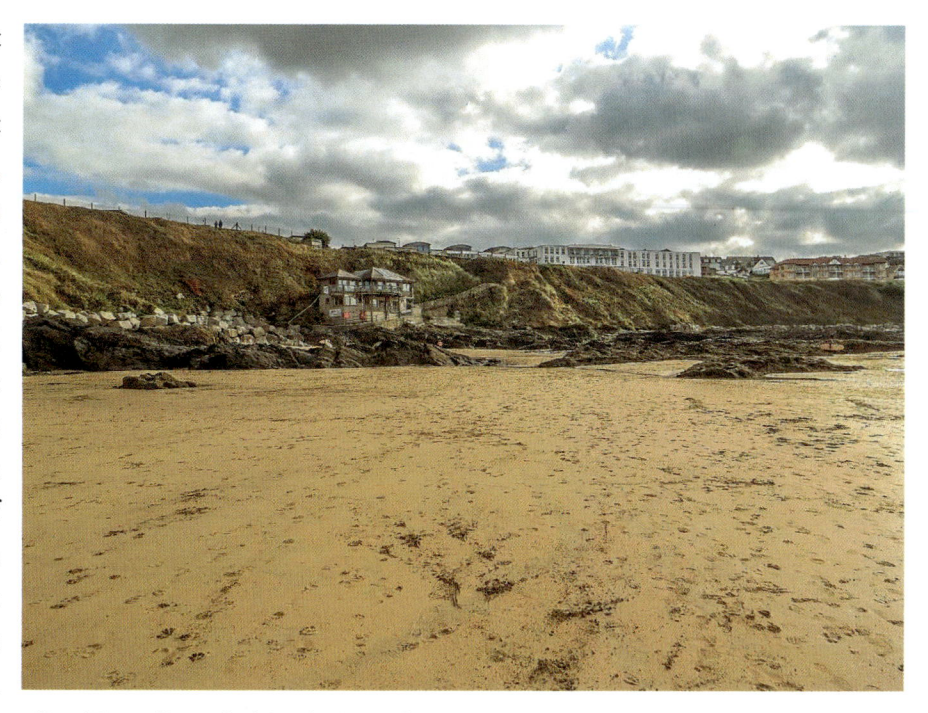

The golf course behind the beach sits on the site of what was once a commercial lead mine, variously known as 'Fistral Mine', 'North Wheal Providence', and finally as 'Newquay Consols'. Silver and lead ores were taken across the Gannel for smelting at a works on the south bank of the river. The mine closed in 1890 and its spoil heaps were used to fill in the shafts before the site was contoured to create an 18-hole links course. It's impossible to miss the distinctive *Headland Hotel* overlooking the northern end of the beach, the creation of Silvanus Trevail, an architect and pioneer of tourism who had already designed a number of hotels in the town when he came up with the idea of building another on this prominent headland in the late 19th century. Unfortunately, local farmers used the land for grazing, and fishermen claimed the site was common land where they had dried their nets for generations. Heated arguments ensued and this was the beginning of what came to be known as the 'Newquay Riots' which saw workmen threatened and fires started, while an angry mob trashed the foundation walls and scaffolding before tipping the foreman's hut into the sea. When Trevail paid a visit he was pelted with eggs and apples, pinned against a railing and subjected to, as the press reported, "a very fierce outpouring of contempt and insolent abuse." Eventually, 200 out-of-work Cornish miners were drafted in to complete the building but associated plans to develop the rest of Fistral common were abandoned. The hotel opened in June 1900. Edward VII and Queen Alexandra were the first of various royals to stay at the hotel, with Prince Charles and Princess Anne enjoying several visits. Many TV shows and films have been shot there, notably the 1990 production of Roald Dahl's *The Witches*, starring Angelica Houston and Rowan Atkinson.

Fistral is not without its faults: the sheer popularity of the beach, especially when hosting events, has led to damage to the dunes, while the land on which the surfing complex was built has a history of erosion and the car park was laid on an area of flattened dunes. Because of this they are both prone to being inundated with sand and, to counter the threat, ugly gabions and rock armour have been positioned in front of them as protection. That apart, it's a fine beach with wonderful waves and no visit to Newquay is complete without experiencing it, although it might be advisable to be elsewhere when *Boardmasters* is on!

39. RIVER GANNEL
SW 796 611
P, PT, DA

There are many reasons to love the River Gannel, and not the least is that it brings the southwards sprawl of Newquay to a sudden stop, forcing the developers to look elsewhere for their next land grab. The river rises by the village of Indian Queens and flows northwards until it passes under the old packhorse bridge at Trevemper, thereafter becoming a delightful tidal estuary with several areas of salt marsh on both sides of the main river channel. At low water the exposed mudflats make the ideal habitat for wading birds to feed on shellfish, worms and crabs, and up to 5,000 birds have been recorded sheltering here during harsh winters, including dunlin, ringed plover, grey plover, greenshank, redshank, widgeon and teal.

The name of the river comes from the Cornish *gan heyl*, 'mouth of estuary or saltings', and it's this part where the receding tide sees the flowing water reduced to a meandering stream as a delightful sandy beach emerges around it, stretching for over a mile until it joins the glorious beach at Crantock. One of the more magical experiences of Cornwall is to walk from Newquay to Crantock via the pristine but undulating soft sand of the newly uncovered Gannel, with two footbridges allowing access over the stream to the drier patches of sand; at Trenance the bridge is covered for about an hour either side of high tide whereas the Penpol bridge is covered for about 2½ hours either side. Don't take any risks when attempting to cross: the dangers are encapsulated in a folk tale of the crying of gulls being the souls of those who died attempting to cross when the tide came rushing in and, confused by the whirling water, they were swept beneath the waves by the powerful current.

By low water there are sandy areas on both sides of the river, and, being more sheltered than the exposed Crantock Beach, they can become busy during the summer, the favourite area being below the dunes on the seaward side of Penpol Creek. There is, of course, barely any beach at high water, perhaps just a narrow strip on the southern side, and be aware that the tide comes in unbelievably quickly. Even in shallow water the current can be extremely powerful and the low banks of sand are quickly flooded. It's important, therefore, to plan your visit around the tide times. Watching the tide rush in from a safe spot high on the riverbank is a magical sight that shouldn't be missed, with eddies and whirlpools forming as the water surges upstream. Those strong currents make it unsafe for swimming, especially on an ebbing tide, no matter how tempting it might appear. Paddling in the shallows is fine, though, and very popular, although the further away from the mouth the safer it is. The many sand pools that are left behind are a more than adequate recompense for the absence of rock pools. At high water the sheltered nature of the river makes it perfect for kayaks and SUPs. There's no safety equipment or lifeguards but both can be found on Crantock Beach, the latter during the summer only. *Trenance Stables* use the bridleway and parts of the foreshore for regular group horse riding. Dogs are allowed all year. Refreshments can be obtained from *Fern Pit Café*, established in 1910, on the north side of the river, with a terraced tea garden providing wonderful views of the estuary and Crantock Beach. They also operate a passenger ferry across the river, which operates for approximately three hours either side of high water from the end of May until mid-September, 10am-6pm. The nearest toilets are in Crantock Beach car park. Other car parks can be found on Pentire Point East, followed by a short walk along Riverside Crescent to the steps that lead to the *Fern Pit Café* and ferry, and on Tregunnel Hill with a walk along the foreshore or road to follow. There is a regular bus service from Newquay to Crantock.

The Tregunnel car park is next to the site of Reed's Boatyard where, in the 19th century, ships of up to 250 tons were built, with launches taking place during spring tides to much fanfare. Smaller boats are still moored and repaired in the area. The boatyard was just part of what was once a very busy river, dating back to the Middle Ages when it acted as a port for what is now Newquay, before the harbour was built. In the 18th and 19th centuries coal for the Truro smelting works was unshipped at Penpol Creek; remains of the quay at Penpol are still visible at low water, as are the remains of a lime kiln where limestone was unloaded and burnt before being spread on the land to improve soil quality. Other vessels moored at Fern Pit where their cargoes were transferred to shallow-draught barges to be carried on the flood tide up to Trevemper. On the southern shore there was a lead and silver smelting works, while on the Newquay side, at Trethellan, there was a 19th century lead mine discharging water onto the beach via an adit. The lead from the mine was initially smelted across the river until it became more economical to export the ore to South Wales. Trethellan was also the site of a Bronze Age village and an Iron Age burial site.to export the ore to South Wales. Trethellan was also the site of a Bronze Age village and an Iron Age burial site.

The river is known for the legend of the Gannel Crake, an eerie, unearthly cry, described in the 19th century as being like "a thousand voices pent up in misery, with one long wail dying away in the distance." The superstitious regard it as the cry of a troubled spirit that forever haunts the river, while others suggest it's the wailing of a 'wrecker' who, crossing the river on a rare mission of mercy, was swept out to sea and drowned. In contrast, the less imaginative attempt to explain it as the cry of a rare bird or the inrush of water in a nearby cavern. Today, the river is home to an abundance of wildlife, from wading birds such as egrets, to fish such as bass and sea trout, and the peace and quiet is likely to be disrupted only by the chattering cry of wildfowl or the distant rumbling of the sea. The timing of any visit to the Gannel is all-important – it's best to arrive a couple of hours before low water, although the view from the dunes of Crantock Beach provide splendid compensation for those who arrive too early.

40. CRANTOCK
SW 787 611
P, PT, SF, SW, L, DA

After the lively bustle of Newquay a visit to the picturesque village of Crantock is like entering a different country or, as some would have it, re-entering Cornwall. The village is centred around a medieval animal pound, now known as the Round Garden, and a Grade 1 Listed church, built in the Norman period on the site of an oratory founded by St Carantoc following his arrival in the 5th century. Believed to be a son of the King of Cardiganshire, Carantoc eschewed his royal duties in favour of a more austere religious life, sailing to Ireland to study under St Patrick before setting out to spread the Christian message. In 460 he sailed into the Gannel, along with a large group of Irish hermits who, presumably, quickly went their separate ways. A Celtic monastery was soon established here, later becoming a College of Priests renowned for its learning, the charter being granted by Edward the Confessor. At that time the village was known as *Langorroc,* which seems to translate as 'church site of Correk', possibly a pet-form of Carantoc, although some scholars suggest 'dwelling of monks'. By 1546, though, it had become the more familiar *Crantocke.*

Crantock Beach sweeps gloriously from the mouth of the River Gannel in the east to Vugga Cove in the west, a distance of well over 800yds at low water. North-westerly facing, the flat, golden sand is backed for the most part by an area of sand dunes known as Rushy Green, and the strip of sand beneath them, perhaps 50yds deep in places, is the only area accessible at high water. The ebbing tide, though, retreats for over 600yds, expanding westwards where additional shelter is provided by the surrounding cliffs, although it's important to keep an eye on the tides when in this area, especially if exploring the caves that are exposed. Hidden in one tiny cave is a fascinating carving of a woman's face, accompanied by a poem carved into the stone:

> "Mar not my face but let me be,
> Secure in this lone cavern by the sea,
> Let the wild waves around me roar,
> Kissing my lips for evermore."

It's said that the carvings were inspired by the story of a woman who, sometime in the 1920s, was riding her horse along the beach and somehow became trapped in this cave by the incoming tide. Tragically, both the woman and horse were drowned and the woman's distraught husband or lover made these carvings in remembrance of her. How much truth there is in the tale is unknown; what is known is that the carvings were made by an artist, Joseph Prater, and that there were several drownings on the beach around that time – the tide was just as dangerous in those days – but whether he knew any of the victims is uncertain. The small carving of a horse was added in the 1940s by James Dyer, the local blacksmith, who was tasked with re-etching the carvings after time and graffiti had made them less distinct. The sand level in the cave varies a lot so it's possible the carvings will be above head height on one visit and around waist height the next. The only rock pools will be on the western side, around Vugga Cove. The offshore islet is known as 'The Goose'.

The storms of recent winters, notably Storm Emma in 2018, have resulted in changes to the topography of the beach with the dunes suffering significant erosion, resulting in the formation of 32ft sand cliffs where formerly there were access paths to the beach, and the exposure of barbed wire used as a defence against invasion during WW2. More damage was done to the course of the River Gannel, which formerly hugged the cliffs at the eastern end of the beach when it was guided by a breakwater, built in the early 20th century. Unfortunately, the storms caused a build up of sand, making the breakwater ineffective and resulting in the river diverting to follow its natural course of flowing across the beach before entering the sea. As a result, at low water, bathers must cross the river to reach the sea and it's also led to the creation of a number of channels and gullies, which at certain stages of the tide can contain some very powerful rip currents. It's possible that the breakwater will be rebuilt at some point, channelling the river back towards the cliffs, but there would always be a chance that further storms could, in such a dynamic environment, result in the same problem reoccurring. Swimming should never be undertaken near the river, and the heavy surf, Atlantic swell, and strong rip currents make it dangerous across the beach; RNLI Lifeguards patrol during the summer and swimming is advisable only when and where they designate it to be safe. Safety equipment can be found in the beach car park.

Crantock is an excellent surfing beach and tends to be less busy than the nearby Newquay beaches. The lifeguards operate a designated surfing area, while *The Big Green Surf School* is based behind the beach and all their instructors are qualified lifeguards; they also offer SUP tours along the Gannel estuary, and have a weekly kids' club throughout the summer holidays, allowing parents a welcome break. Dogs are welcome all year provided they are kept under control. Toilets are situated in the beach car park, in the village, and at West Pentire.

There are two large car parks close to the beach, both with a capacity of around 200 cars, with the National Trust one tucked right behind the sand dunes. There's another car park in the village of West Pentire at the west end of the beach. Crantock is on the Newquay to Truro bus route with a walk from the bus stop of around 800yds to the Coast Path and dunes via Green Lane, or 640yds to the beach car park via Beach Road. When part of this road was dug up to lay water mains it unearthed dozens of skulls, skeletons, and coffin-slates; apparently the blown sand which once covered this area was ideal for burying victims of the Black Death.

There are a number of access points to the beach with several paths over the dunes, but most people favour the wide, flat path from the corner of the NT car park, which is suitable for pushchairs as it avoids the dunes. From West Pentire it's necessary to follow the Coast Path eastwards to Pusey's Steps, which lead down to the beach but are only accessible at low water. At other times continue along the path until reaching the dunes, a distance of just over 750yds. The best way to reach the beach, though, is by walking from Newquay along the Gannel whenever the tide permits, a magical experience, with a short trip on the ferry from Fern Pit as a fine alternative for roughly three hours either side of high water.

Ice creams and light refreshments are available on the beach during the summer months and there's a seasonal café and beach shop in the higher beach car park, with the *Fern Pit Café* handily placed across the Gannel estuary. The village itself has a small shop and two pubs, *The Cornishman* and, near the church, the 400 year old, thatch-roofed *Old Albion*. Under the stone floor of the pub is a secret chamber that was used by smugglers and there's still a tunnel that connects to the beach, although it's now blocked for safety reasons. Perched on the West Pentire headland is the *C-Bay Café/Bar/Bistro*, which opened in 2013, with the much older *Bowgie Inn* nearby, *bowgie* translating as 'cowshed', which is appropriate as it was formerly a farm. Voted Best British Beach by BBC Coast in 2013, Crantock's combination of wild beauty and family friendliness fully warrants that accolade and, in combination with the Gannel, it should be on everyone's list of places to visit.

41. PORTH JOKE or POLLY JOKE
SW 772 604
RP, SF, DA

Nestling unobtrusively between the popular beaches of Crantock and Holywell Bay, Porth Joke is a wonderfully unspoilt sandy beach set amidst some of the most idyllic coastal scenery that Cornwall has to offer. It's nowhere near as famous as its neighbours, mainly due to being blissfully inaccessible to cars, but it is a favourite of the locals, especially in summer when other beaches can be excessively crowded. The author Winston Graham loved this area, and Nampara Cove in his *Poldark* novels was based on a composite of Porth Joke and the tiny Vugga Cove on the west side of Crantock Beach.

To begin with the bewildering name, it's believed to derive from the Cornish *Pol Lejouack*, 'Jackdaw cove', although others suggest *Porth Lojowek*, 'cove rich in plants'. The latter would refer to an astonishing 154 species of wildflower that flourish in the surrounding fields throughout spring and early summer, when the headland to the east, Pentire Point West, can be ablaze with poppies and corn marigold, much to the delight of photographers. The north-westerly facing beach nestles between turf covered headlands with Kelsey Head to the west, and backs onto a shallow valley that leads to Cubert Common, an undulating area of sandy grassland. There's a legend that *Langona* or *Langarrow*, a town with 7 churches, lies buried here and in the adjoining dunes as a punishment by God for the greed and dissolute behaviour of its populace! Nowadays it's owned by the National Trust and popular with walkers and horse riders. Kelsey Head is the site of a cliff castle and burial mounds, while flints and pieces of pottery have been unearthed there. Just south of the headland are three enclosed fields, probably medieval, known as The Kelseys.

Porth Joke is an inlet beach and it shares many of the features found at similar beaches, being deeper than it is wide, while the tide retreats a long way, in this case more than 450yds, unveiling a wonderful, flat beach of coarse sand, almost triangular in shape when the tide is fully out. At this time numerous rock pools and caves await exploration, while, on the western side, there are a number of craggy inlets, often sheltered and offering seclusion on those summer days when the beach is at its busiest. Be aware, though, that the returning tide comes in quickly. There's the added bonus of a small stream running across the beach, while just off Kelsey Head is an islet, The Chick, home to fulmars and seals, with the latter often seen popping up just offshore. High water sees a small crescent of sand usually survive at the back of the beach, although there's more shingle in the winter and a combination of stormy weather and high spring tides can sometimes see the whole beach engulfed. There are no dog restrictions but be aware that there is often plenty of livestock in the surrounding fields, and occasionally on the beach itself.

 Due to the heavy swell and strong rip currents it's not suitable for swimming, the only exception being in very calm conditions on a rising high tide, but it is popular with surfers, although not as busy as the neighbouring beaches. Be aware that the incoming tide is strong as the inlet funnels the water, allowing the opportunity to enjoy some bigger waves. Safety equipment can be found at the back of the beach but there are no lifeguard patrols. Part of the charm of Porth Joke is the complete absence of any development, which means there are no facilities, with the nearest seasonal toilets found in West Pentire car park and the nearest refreshments available from the *Bowgie Inn*, also in West Pentire. There are two car parks to choose from, both about a 700yd walk from the beach, one in West Pentire and a smaller one in a field near Treago Mill, reached by a public byway from Treago Farm campsite. They are lovely walks that add to the enjoyment of a day at Porth Joke, while the walks along the Coast Path from both Crantock and Holywell are, if anything, even more thrilling, although longer. Definitely a beach that has to be visited!

42. HOLYWELL BAY
SW 765 590
P, PT, SF, SW, L, DA

Holywell Bay has garnered a legion of new fans in recent years thanks to the BBC's *Poldark*, with many scenes featuring Ross and Demelza gazing wistfully out to sea or galloping on horseback across the long sandy shore. Not that it needed the publicity – it has long been one of Cornwall's most popular beaches. At low water there's almost ¾ of a mile of golden sand stretching between Kelsey Head in the east and Penhale Point in the west, while the sea retreats for around 350 yards to expose a huge flat beach. At high water there's still a 700yd long strip of sand, much of it backed by an impressive sand dune system that provides plenty of sheltered hollows in which to escape the crowds. Lying offshore are the bay's most distinctive features, the pyramid shaped islets known as Carter's Rocks or, less originally, Gull Rocks, while a delightful stream meanders behind the sand dunes and hugs the cliffs before fanning out as it approaches the sea, perfect for paddling, splashing or fishing nets. Although there are no rock pools, the ebbing tide usually leaves behind enough sand pools to bring more delight to children. Sitting subtly at the foot of the dunes is the Surf Lifesaving Clubhouse, which often has to be dug out of the sand after the wild weather of winter.

Strong currents and the powerful Atlantic swell mean that swimming is only advisable when RNLI Lifeguards are present in the summer, although it's sometimes possible to bathe on a rising high tide in calm conditions. It's a very popular surfing beach, suitable for all levels of ability, with a surf school operating from the beach and another based in one of the nearby holiday camps. During the peak summer months the lifeguards operate a segregated area for surfing and bodyboarding, but the most experienced surfers tend to favour the westerly side of the beach when there is a large swell. Safety equipment can be found by the clubhouse.

There are roadside parking restrictions during the summer but there is a large National Trust car park just across the road from one of the access paths to the beach, while the village is on the Truro - Newquay bus route. There are several paths to the beach with the one from the centre of the village, by the shop, being the shortest, although they all involve crossing the stream at least once, either by bridge or paddling. The wonderful sand dunes keep the beach out of view, with just the occasional tantalising glimpse depending on the route taken, until eventually the huge stretch of sand is revealed in all its glory. Much of the beach on the westerly side of the stream cannot be seen at first sight, being backed by high cliffs rather than sand dunes; at this end of the beach care needs to be taken not to get cut off by the fast incoming tide. Dogs are allowed all year.

Holywell was little more than a few cottages with farming and mining as the mainstay for the population, but now it is totally devoted to the holiday trade with several caravan and camping sites. There are two seasonal shops in the village and two pubs, one of them thatched. Nearby there's an 18 hole par 3 golf course and a pitch and put course. Toilets are located on the road close to the car park. In 1939 the MoD established Penhale Army Camp on the cliffs to the west and it remained in operation until 2010 when it was deemed surplus to requirements and sold to a developer who plans to build 134 homes on the site, despite opposition from the local community. The cliffs used to have spectacular engine houses on them for the silver and lead mines which dotted the area, but they were demolished by the army during WW2 as they were considered to be landmarks for German bombers. All that remain are a number of adits which pockmark the cliff, and the former Count House, from where the miners were paid, still perched dramatically on the cliff above Hoblyn's Cove.

Although Holywell is always busy during the summer the majority of visitors tend to favour the centre and western half of the beach. Walk eastwards along the shore and it's much quieter, with the added bonus of the rusted remains of a shipwreck to be spotted near the low water mark: in October 1917 an Argentinian ship, *Francia,* was carrying coal from Port Talbot to France when it was stranded here. Much of the ship was salvaged but the rest had to be left behind and it has remained here ever since. It's by continuing eastwards, to the cliffs below Kelsey Head, where the secret gem of Holywell can be found, as well as the explanation for its name. There are several tempting caves to explore but the one to seek out looks like a narrow slit in the rock close to the low water mark. Check the tide times if visiting because it very quickly becomes cut off, but entering the cave is like discovering a new world. It's best to take a torch to shed light on this dark and mysterious grotto, and it reveals multi-coloured calcareous rocks – pink, red, purple, white and green – down which tumbles a cascade of fresh water, carving out natural stepped basins: this is the holy well that gives the bay its name. The

17th century name was *Porth Elyn*, 'cove of the clear stream', but by the end of the 18th century it was recorded as Holywell. It's possible to follow the steps up into a tiny cavern, although care needs to be taken as they are invariably covered with slimy green weed and the sand level inside the cave can vary considerably. It has a definite pre-Christian feel, and it's known that mothers used to immerse their ailing children in the healing water, but the canny 7th century saint – Cubert – would almost certainly have used it for baptisms; your author risked a sip of the water and lived to tell the tale! There is also a second holy well on land owned by one of the holiday camps, on the edge of the golf course.

Despite its proximity to Newquay and its popularity as a family-friendly and surfing beach, Holywell Bay has been spared the horrors of commercialisation thanks to its owners, The National Trust. Unsurprisingly then, this wild and beautiful beach has appeared many times on screen including, as well as *Poldark*, commercials, TV series such as the BBC's 2014 version of *Jamaica Inn*, and films such as *Die Another Day* (2002) and *Summer in February* (2013). It's a magical place with something for everyone, and every beach lover should ensure they pay it a visit.

43. PENHALE SANDS
P, SF, SW, L, DR

Penhale Sands stretches for 1.6 miles from Ligger Point in the north to Cotty's Point in the south, where it links up with Perranporth Beach to form a glorious expanse of golden sand, known as Perran or Ligger Bay, which continues as far as Droskyn Point, a total distance of 2.2 miles. When the tide is out a large expanse of wonderful flat sand is exposed, over 400yds deep in places, with the majority backed by imposing dunes. Although larger, it's always much quieter than Perranporth, especially at its northern end where the steep, undulating sand dunes isolate it from the bustling resort town. The dunes formed over 5,000 years ago and are the largest dune system in Cornwall, consisting of Penhale Sands, Gear Sands and Reen Sands. At first glance it seems a barren landscape but it's actually home to a wide range of flora, including many rare species, and provides an ideal habitat for wildlife, including 27 species of butterfly and 107 species of moth. Towards the southern end of the dunes are two sprawling holiday camps, while a large slice of the northern part belongs to Penhale Army Camp. This secluded end of the beach is popular with naturists, but for many years the MoD complained about this practice until a compromise was reached in 2007, and now nude sunbathing is permitted on the beach but not in the dunes. There are no rock pools and dog restrictions apply during the summer. In July 2016 a 40ft sperm whale died after becoming stranded on the beach, too injured to be saved. It was the first confirmed female sperm whale recorded in UK for over 100 years.

The beach is believed to have been the landing place in the 6th century for one of Cornwall's most important saints, Piran, the patron saint of tinners and of Cornwall, although St Petroc could also lay claim to the latter. Hidden in a hollow in the dunes are the remains of his oratory, thought to be the oldest Christian site in Cornwall and one of the oldest in Britain. In the 10th century the oratory was abandoned after being overwhelmed by sand, and a replacement built a ¼ mile inland on the far side of a river, in the belief that sand couldn't cross running water. This, too, was abandoned in 1795 and a new church built further inland. The oratory was rediscovered and excavated in the 18th century and then encased in a large concrete structure for protection from the ever-shifting sands. In 2014 the sand and concrete were removed to reveal the remains to be in a good state of preservation. Much of the medieval church had been dismantled and reused in the later building but in 2005 it too was excavated, revealing masonry dating from the late 12th or early 13th century. According to legend the lost town of *Langona* lies buried beneath the dunes, stretching as far as Cubert Common, near to Porth Joke.

There is a small parking area in the dunes, reached by driving through *Perran Sands Holiday Park*. A sandy path leads from the car park to one of the easier access points to the beach; other paths end in steep scrambles from the dunes. The walk back up the dunes to the car park has frequently been described as 'knackering!' There is also a path from the holiday park which, although steep in places, is more suitable for families, and leads to a section of beach patrolled by RNLI Lifeguards during the summer - their lookout hut is tucked under the cliffs by Cotty's Point. It's possible to park in Perranporth with a walk along the beach to follow, although at high water the sea reaches the foot of the cliffs at Cotty's Point, making a detour through the dunes necessary to reach the strip of sand that is usually present at all stages of the tide. Bus users can walk from either Perranporth or from the holiday camp, which is visited by buses during the summer and stop just outside at other times.

Strong rip currents mean that swimming should only be undertaken in the area designated as safe by the lifeguards when they are on duty during the summer. They don't patrol the remote northern end of the beach and there is no safety equipment there, the nearest being situated by the access path near the lifeguard hut. It's a popular surfing beach, having more swell than Perranporth, with experienced surfers tending to congregate at the northern end, known as Penhale Corner, while beginners and the inexperienced should keep to the southern, resort, end in the area designated by the lifeguards. A surf school operates out of *Perran Sands Holiday Camp*. The long, straight beach is also perfect for kite-surfing.

Wild, beautiful, and with an atmosphere of mystery and myth, Penhale Sands can be enjoyed at any time of the year, and at the height of the summer season it's vast enough to provide sanctuary from the crowds that flock to Perranporth and Holywell Bay.

44. PERRANPORTH
SW 756 545
P, PT, RP, SF, SW, L, DA

Perranporth Beach makes up the southern section of Ligger or Perran Bay, joining up with Penhale Sands to form a 2.2 mile stretch of glorious golden sand. It's a hugely popular beach and at the height of summer can be very crowded, especially at high water when there is still a large area of sand from the main access point by Beach Road to Cotty's Point, the small headland to the north. Much of this area is backed by Reen Sands, the southernmost part of the huge dune system we encountered at Penhale. The Surf Lifesaving Club is in this part of the beach, as is *The Watering Hole*, which claims to be the only bar situated on a beach in the UK, making it handy for refreshments; the bar has made the news in recent years when winter storms shifted swathes of sand from the beach, leaving *The Watering Hole* perched precariously on its own little island of sand. As the tide retreats a large expanse of flat sand is exposed, broken only by two streams that converge and flow across the beach at its southern end. At low water it's a wonderful beach, suitable for all the family, some 700yds deep, with the vast expanse of Penhale Sands stretching to the north, while to the south, towards Droskyn Point, there are numerous outcrops, stacks, and natural arches beneath the rugged cliffs. Beyond Droskyn is a more remote area, good for escaping from the crowds and the site of innumerable rock pools and caves, some of them man made, others natural and formerly used by smugglers to land their contraband out of sight of the Customs men. In 1780 a secret smuggling syndicate was set up by some of the leading men of the village, including the local vicar and Methodist minister. They acquired a fast ship to allow them swift access to Cherbourg, France, brazenly naming the vessel *Cherbourg*. Under the cover of darkness *Cherbourg* would be met by smaller boats for the transfer of goods, which were then taken to various secret landing spots. At Droskyn Point there were two very large caves, big enough to take several rowing boats at a time, and a shaft was cut from the roof of one of the caves to the surface to allow contraband to be hauled up by rope and pulley. Men would be standing by with mules to spirit the bounty away. There are more caves on the other side of the beach near Cotty's Point.

Surrounded by sand in the middle of the beach is the 50ft high Chapel Rock, scene of many a childhood adventure. It features a natural bathing pool where the water often reaches Mediterranean temperatures on sunny summer afternoons; the pool was created in 1958 as a safe place for children to learn to swim. Be aware, though, that the tide comes in swiftly around the rock, as well as quickly covering the beach beneath the cliffs. Perranporth is notorious for dangerous rip currents, especially at low water and around Chapel Rock during an ebbing tide; therefore, apart from the pool, it's best to swim only when RNLI Lifeguards are present - they designate separate safe areas for bathing and surfing, the latter being very popular here. The more experienced surfers tend to head for Droskyn Point and the southern end of the beach where there are often sizeable waves, while for beginners there are three surf schools to choose from, *Ticket to Ride*, *Perranporth*, and another based at *The Watering Hole*. There are a number of safety equipment points, while members of the *Surf Lifesaving Club*, formed in the 1950s following a spate of accidents, supplement the work of the lifeguards.

Dogs are allowed all year but must be kept on a lead during July and August. There are toilets adjacent to the two main car parks and also behind *The Watering Hole*. Access is easy and suitable for prams and wheelchairs, from the Promenade car park (capacity 130 cars) next to the beach. There's a larger car park at the top of Cliff Road, where there is also a limited amount of roadside parking, with access to the beach down a flight of steps. Buses from Newquay and Truro stop by the Promenade car park.

Visitors to Perranporth will have difficulty believing that this bustling resort town was once a small village dominated by engine houses, dressing floors and waste heaps of the mining industry, with fishing and farming being the other occupations. The principal mine was Wheal Leisure, which operated from the 16th century through to the mid-19th century, and fans of *Poldark* will recognise this as the name of Ross Poldark's mine in the series. The author of the novels, Winston Graham, lived in Perranporth for 34 years and was greatly influenced by area's history of mining, fishing, and smuggling. There's even an area of Perranporth called Nampara, and Graham himself lived in Nampara Lodge,

107

which later became a hotel before being demolished due to subsidence. The last major catch of pilchards in the village was in 1906, while the last mine, Treamble Iron Mine, closed in 1952. By then Perranporth was already an established tourist destination following the arrival of the railway in 1903, which ran from Chacewater via St Agnes. In its heyday there was a train from Paddington to Perranporth every Saturday during the summer season, with local trains running to Truro and Newquay. The line closed in 1963. Today, Perranporth is almost completely devoted to the tourist industry and, at its peak season worst, takes on the character of a mini-Newquay when the car parks are full and the streets gridlocked with traffic; happily, other times of the year are more peaceful, with a touch of elegance being provided by the flower and palm tree gardens that surround the clock tower, and the boating lake in Boscawen Gardens. It has everything expected of a modern resort with plenty of shops, cafés, restaurants and pubs, plus hotels, guest houses and, tucked away in the dunes, a couple of holiday camps. Best of all, though, is its glorious beach, which has something for everyone and is guaranteed to bring joy to all who visit it.

45. TREVELLAS PORTH
SW 725 518
P, RP, SF, SW, DA

Trevellas Porth is the first and lesser known of two beaches close to St Agnes, a village dominated by the relics of the mining industry that thrived here throughout the 19th century. The beach lies at the mouth of Trevellas Coombe, one of two valleys that run down from the village to the sea. The name was first recorded in 1302 as the site of the Trevellas family manor, but it's sometimes called the Blue Hills due to the colour of the slate found there. There is a long history of mining in the valley, beginning with streaming for alluvial tin, and by the late 1800s almost the entire area was covered with huge sheds and ore dressing machinery, while chimneys belched out black smoke and the noise from machinery was deafening. The most prominent ruins are the engine house and stack of the old Blue Hills Mine, which was active between 1813 and 1898, and in 1974 reopened as a small-scale tin producer using tin ore from the seabed that washes ashore at Trevellas Porth. Now called *Blue Hills Tin Streams,* it's open between April and October and offers tours that provide an insight into the ancient skills of the tinners, as well as having beautiful hand-crafted gifts for sale. Whether visiting *Blue Hills* or not, the walk through the now tranquil valley is beautiful, with the silence of the mining ruins standing as a melancholy monument to the generations who laboured there. The one exception to this serenity occurs every Easter when the Blue Hills play host to a leg of the Land's End Classic Trial, organised by the Motorcycling Club, when up to 400 vintage motorcycles and cars tackle the undulating tracks and paths around the valley.

Approaching the beach the eye is drawn to the rocky stacks of Bawden Rocks, also known as 'Cow and Calf' or 'Man and his Man', which stand about 1½ miles offshore. The larger rock rises to about 80ft above the high water mark and provides a nesting ground for razorbills, shags, and guillemots. An annual festival is held at nearby Trevaunance Cove featuring numerous competitions including a swim from the rocks, with the competitors ferried out to them by boat. At high water Trevellas is mainly stones and shingle with perhaps an occasional patch of sand, but the ebbing tide reveals a good area of sand, around 140yds wide. At low water a reef of flat rock platforms is unveiled along with more rocks to the west, both ideal for rock pools. It's sometimes possible to scramble over the westerly rocks to Trevaunance Cove and, if doing so, keep an eye out for mineral veins in the cliff that contain pyrite, gold sparkling crystals often referred to as 'fool's gold'. Be aware, though, that the cliffs at the back of the beach are susceptible to rock falls. The stream that once provided power for the mines now trickles across the centre of the beach. Unpredictable currents make swimming dangerous at low water, but it's much safer at high water in calm conditions. Similarly, snorkelling is only possible in the same conditions when it can be breathtakingly good on the western side of the beach. Rock outcrops make surfing unfeasible at low water but it is possible for experienced surfers from mid-tide onwards. Safety equipment can be found above the beach. Dogs are allowed all year but there are no toilets or other facilities, the nearest being at Trevaunance Cove. Surprisingly for such an unspoilt cove there is a small parking area just above the beach, reached by following a very narrow road to Cross Coombe, followed by an even narrower track. Alternatively, park at Trevaunance Cove and walk from there, either by following the Coast Path or by a deceptively lengthy scramble over the rocks at low water.

On the cliffs to the east is Perranporth Airfield, which saw its first flights in 1924 and in WW2 became an RAF base used by 21 different squadrons, all flying Spitfires. It was decommissioned in April 1946 but remains one of the best examples of a WW2 fighter base still in existence. In 2006 it became home to the *Cornish Parachute Centre* and *Perranporth Flying Club*.

46. TREVAUNANCE COVE
SW 721 515
P, RP, SF, SW, L, DA

Trevaunance Cove, sometimes referred to as St Agnes Beach, lies at the end of a narrow valley that runs down from the village of St Agnes to the sea. St Agnes was a 4th century Christian martyr who doesn't seem to have any connection to the village apart from legends, of which there are many. In the 13th century the village name was *Bryanek*, the meaning of which is unclear. St Agnes has an extremely rich mining history due to the unique high quality tin found here, formed by action between granite and the complex rock found around the area's cliffs. The valleys and cliffs have been worked for many centuries but the industry's boom years were from 1830 until the mid-1870s, with the population of the village peaking at 7,757 in 1841, but the falling price of tin saw many small mines close and the three largest, Wheal Kitty, Polberro, and Wheal Friendly merge, and as a single concern continue to operate until the 1940s. With transport by land difficult, Trevaunance Cove was the obvious choice for a harbour to service the local mines, even though there had been at least four failed attempts from 1632 onwards when harbours built to aid local fishermen were all destroyed by the stormy sea. In 1798, though, a north quay wall was built and shipping trade flourished to such an extent that a shorter south wall was added and the north wall extended, leaving an entrance less than 9yds wide, making access difficult even in calm seas. The harbour was only big enough to contain a maximum of 6 coasting ships, and apart from a narrow flight of steps and ladders there was no access to the quays from land. Instead, cargo had to be hauled up the cliffs by horse whims, and loaded onto the ships by two long chutes, with mainly coal being imported and copper ore exported to Wales for smelting. Other industries also benefited from the harbour with a pilchard seine established in 1802 and large fish cellars built, but, despite some large catches in 1829/30, it was never particularly successful. In the 19th century there was a significant shipbuilding business in the cove, peaking between 1873 and 1879 when 4 sizeable schooners were built. The harbour survived intact until the summer of 1915 when one stone in the North Quay was washed away; the damage wasn't repaired and an autumn gale breached the wall. By 1924 the whole harbour was completely destroyed, reduced to a heap of granite blocks, a mass of which can still be seen at low water on the westerly side of the beach.

The cove is best viewed from the Coast Path, heading west towards Chapel Porth, from where it's easy to see how nature has reclaimed the once heavily industrialised landscape, with the high, rugged cliffs nobly bearing the scars of the mining industry. It's a northerly facing beach, mainly sandy with patches of shingle, and with rocky areas on both sides. At low water it expands to around 225yds deep and 190yds wide, with the rocky areas making it seem even bigger. The surrounding cliffs provide shelter from westerly winds, while a small stream that fans out across the sand is usually irresistible for children. In winter the sand can be sprinkled with small stones. Plenty of pools can be found in the rocky areas towards the sea, best on low spring tides. There's an awkward scramble over the rocks eastwards to Trevellas Porth, which is usually much quieter than the family-friendly Trevaunance. Dogs are allowed all year but should be kept on a lead, and there's easy access to the beach via a slipway from the end of the road, adjacent to a boat slipway which can be used for launching small craft, although it's not very practical when the beach is busy with summer visitors. There's also a long flight of steps down the cliffs to the beach on the western side. A handful of boats are frequently hauled up by the slipway as a small fishing fleet still operates from the cove. Timing a visit to Trevaunance is important as there's usually no beach at high water, although there may be a thin strip of shingle and sand at neap tides.

Strong currents make swimming dangerous, particularly at low water, although it's sometimes possible at high water in calm conditions. It's better, though, to swim only when RNLI Lifeguards patrol the beach during the summer, keeping to the area they designate as safe. Surfing can be reasonable but it's generally a lot calmer than Chapel Porth or Porthtowan, making it perfect for beginners, with lessons available from *Breakers Surf School*. When conditions are favourable it can be very popular with surfers of all levels. It's not suitable for snorkelling other than on a calm day towards high water when there are interesting areas on both sides of the beach. Safety equipment can be found above the beach. Refreshments are available from *Breakers Beach Café* and *Schooners Bar and Restaurant,* both situated on the quay at the back of the beach. There is also a beach shop, and beach huts are available for hire. The *Driftwood Spars* pub and restaurant is around 200yds up the road. Public toilets can be found on the left-hand side of the road around 100yds from the beach. There are two car parks within 300yds of the beach but their combined capacity of around 150 cars is insufficient to cope with summer demand and there is very little roadside parking allowed. The nearest bus stop is Peterville on the B3285, just over half a mile along Quay Road from the beach.

47. CHAPEL PORTH
SW 697 495
P, RP, SF, SW, L, DA

Set in the heart of St Agnes Mining District at the mouth of a long, deep valley, Chapel Porth is a beach of stark contrasts, varying from a narrow rocky inlet at high water to a vast expanse of sand at low. It's owned by the National Trust and is completely unspoilt, with just a car park, toilets, lifeguard hut and a café, all beneficial additions that make this beautiful beach more amenable for visitors. The car park was formerly the site of a stamping mill driven by a 20ft diameter water wheel, positioned by the wall next to the present day toilets, and the whole of the valley, Chapel Coombe, and the surrounding cliffs, were once intensively worked by mines bearing names such as East Charlotte, Wheal Friendly and Wheal Coates, with the iconic Towanroath engine house standing guard on the cliffs above the beach. Only one narrow and, in places, fairly steep road links with the outside world, winding for 1¾ miles from St Agnes to the car park, which is big enough for 60 cars; during the summer a much bigger car park is available in a field some 600yds up the road. There is no roadside parking. A small slope leads down to the back of the beach, all rocks and pebbles and no more than 50yds wide, and at high water this is all that is accessible. In overcast weather, especially in the winter, it can have a sombre atmosphere with the beach hemmed in by precipitous dark cliffs that echo to the plaintive cries of sea birds, while wild and windy weather sees the north-westerly facing beach completely swamped under the full force of the Atlantic Ocean. It was following such a night of storms that, on the 18th November 1928, the SS *Eltham*, a 687 ton steamer carrying a cargo of coal from Swansea to Rouen, was discovered washed up, just off the beach, with a broken back. There was no sign of any crew and no reports of flares in the night, but several hours later a smashed lifeboat bearing the ship's name was washed ashore in a cove six miles away. Once the storm abated, close examination revealed that apart from a hole in her hull, probably caused by breakers on the shore, there was no other damage, and no log book or papers, while her anchors and chains were stowed away and there was no sign of any cargo. So inexplicable was the fate of the ship that some sailors of the time believed her to have been carried by mysterious vortices and lifted high into the air, shaking all cargo and objects loose, before being dropped at Chapel Porth. Whatever the explanation, the boiler from the wreck remains embedded in the sand, visible at low water. In June 1856 the body of a young elephant was washed up on the beach towards Porthtowan. The poor creature's legs were tied together and it had a rope around its neck; presumably the ship on which it was being transported was wrecked somewhere along the coast.

It's at low water, when the tide recedes beyond the towering cliffs, that the beach is transformed from a cramped, rocky beach to a magnificent expanse of golden sand stretching from Porthtowan in the south to Tubby's Head in the north, a distance of around 1½ miles. There are numerous rock pools, natural arches, and caves to explore, including Towanroath Vugga, a partially man-made cave found directly below the engine house that perches precariously on the cliff above. The cave contains an adit used for draining the mine. Simply walking along the vast expanse of sand, with the breeze and sea spray in your face and deafened by the roar of breaking waves, is a magical and very Cornish experience. It's tempting to keep walking to the extremities but be aware that the high cliffs allow no escape from the onrushing tide, so it's essential to be aware of the tide times and be back at the inlet in good time. Dog restrictions apply throughout the summer.

Strong rip currents mean that swimming is only possible when RNLI Lifeguards are present, and only in the area they designate as safe. In the right conditions it's an excellent surfing beach, very popular with locals and often crowded. It's not ideal for beginners. Bellyboarding is also popular and the World Championships are held here every year, with no wetsuits allowed, only swimsuits and wooden boards. The toilets and café are seasonal, the latter famous for its delicious 'hedgehog' ice cream, wrapped in clotted cream and hazelnuts.

The chapel after which the beach is named, and holy well, both dedicated to St Agnes, were situated just to the north of the inlet. Of medieval origin, the chapel was destroyed in 1789 and its stones reused elsewhere, although substantial earth banks remain intact, along with a small building. The well had disappeared by 1820. The surrounding cliff tops and St Agnes Beacon are among the last remnants of a huge tract of heathland that once spread across Cornwall. This rare and important habitat is internationally recognised for its wealth of wildlife, and from late summer onwards comes alive with colour, forming a brilliant yellow and purple patchwork of gorse and heather.

Every May, Chapel Porth hosts the *Bolster Festival*, re-enacting the legend of a giant, Bolster, who terrorised the local population, including St Agnes. Apparently, Bolster fell in love with Agnes, a young local maiden, who sensed an opportunity to rid the village of the ogre. She demanded that, to prove the extent of his love, he fill a small hole on the cliff edge with his blood, an odd request but Bolster believed the hole to be so small that he could complete the task easily. However, it was actually bottomless, opening into a large sea cave, and the giant lost so much blood that he died and fell into the sea. The 'blood-stained' cave can still be seen today.

 Timing is everything at Chapel Porth but arrive on a falling tide and it quickly becomes a wonderful, family-friendly beach that still retains its distinctive Cornish atmosphere and unspoilt ruggedness. It's definitely a beach to visit.

48. PORTHTOWAN
SW 691 480
P, PT, RP, SF, SW, L, DR

Porthtowan bears many similarities to its neighbour, Chapel Porth, but with the bonus of more amenities in the small, relatively modern village that shelters in the two valleys that converge behind the beach. Once again, a mining heritage is very apparent with several old engine houses perched high on the hillside giving a melancholic atmosphere to the valley, while the most eye-catching building in the village is a former engine house intended for Wheal Lushington Mine but never used and now converted into a spectacular dwelling. Other than that there's little trace of its mining past in the village itself, which first developed as a seaside resort in Victorian and Edwardian times when it became popular with the mining communities of Redruth and Camborne. By the 1990s, though, parts of the village had become run down, suffering from vandalism and other social problems, but since then it has been regenerated and is now thriving with a population of around 1,000 and a strong sense of community, best epitomised by the new village hall and a children's play park, both close to the beach. It has everything the modern holidaymaker requires with a general store, a village pub, *The Unicorn*, a fish and chip shop, an ice-cream parlour and two beachside cafés, the *Blue Bar* and *Porthtowan Beach Café*, and a variety of places to stay. The car park just behind the beach has a capacity of 137 cars and also houses the public toilets, and a little roadside parking is also possible. The village is linked by bus to Newquay, St Agnes, Truro, and Redruth.

Porthtowan is a beach of great contrasts, presenting a family-friendly face on sunny summer days but transforming into a scene of rugged grandeur in the wilds of winter. Like Chapel Porth, at high water it's an inlet beach that expands into a seemingly boundless stretch of fine, pale sand as the tide ebbs. The beach is backed by a small sand dune system, which explains the name, *porth towan*, 'cove of sand dunes', and above the high water mark it's mainly a mixture of shingle and stones, especially in winter. It's flanked by imposing steep cliffs but is more spacious than Chapel Porth, being some 200yds wide at high water. Many people choose to sit in the dunes, which has resulted in serious erosion of the marram grass, and a local community group has been set up to help preserve this fragile and important part of the beach. A stream dissects the dunes and runs across the beach before dispersing as it approaches the sea at low water, while a few rock pools are uncovered on both flanks.

As the tide recedes it becomes possible to walk around the southern headland to Lushington Cove, sandy and surrounded by rugged, vertiginous cliffs, with the triangular shaped Tobban Horse Rock at its far end. In the other direction, for around an hour either side of low water, there's a glorious walk along the sand to Chapel Porth, about ¾ of a mile away, but be aware that the tide comes in quickly along this coast and completely covers the beach beyond the headlands; the high tide mark can be seen on the rocks some 6 to 10ft above the sand. It's vital, therefore, to check the tide times and allow plenty of time to make it back to the inlet. Porthtowan is a frequent winner of the Blue Flag Award and is cleaned daily. Dog restrictions apply during the summer. Although it's owned and managed by Cornwall Council, the beach also benefits from the scrutiny of the charity *Surfers Against Sewage*, which was founded here in 1990 and now fights against sea pollution nationwide. In 1998 a 700lb leatherback turtle was found dying on the beach after swallowing a discarded plastic bag. The turtle was about 80 years old and is now preserved in St Agnes Museum. The remnants of a Plymouth barque, *Rose of Devon*, can occasionally be seen at low spring tides, especially after winter storms scour sand from the beach; she was wrecked in November 1897 with the loss of all hands.

Dangerous rip currents make swimming and bathing hazardous in all but the most benign conditions on a rising high tide, therefore it's best to wait until the RNLI Lifeguards are on patrol during the summer, keeping to the area they designate as safe. There's a splendid alternative to the sea in the shape of a beautiful bathing pool created out of the rocks on the easterly side of the beach, accessible at low water and full of purple, turquoise and bright green seaweed. The *Porthtowan Surf Lifesaving Club* is situated on the westerly side of the beach: it has over 200 members and supplements the work of the RNLI Lifeguards, as well as offering training to all age groups, from under-11s upwards. Safety equipment can be found by the clubhouse and by the entrance to the beach. It's an excellent and very popular surfing beach, with a tendency to be a little too busy in the summer, when the lifeguards operate designated surfing and swimming areas. Experienced surfers are lured here by large winter swells, while the *Pure Blue Surf Academy* provides lessons for beginners and the inexperienced.

Porthtowan is a beach with something for everyone: acres of sand, huge waves, craggy rocks and pools, dramatic cliffs and all the amenities needed to make it a memorable holiday destination. It's the last of the beaches in the St Agnes Mining District and, having visited all four it becomes easy to understand why Winston Graham gave permission for this rugged and beautiful coast, blessed with so many monuments to its mining heritage, to be called *Poldark Country*.

49. PORTREATH
SW 653 453
P, PT, RP, SF, SW, L DR

Portreath developed in the 18th century as a busy port, importing coal from Wales and exporting copper ore from mines in the Redruth and Chacewater area. The harbour we see today originated in 1760, while the quay was extended and an inner basin constructed in 1846, and the New Dock, now known as Little Beach, added in the 1860s. The narrow entrance was quite hazardous and tremendous skill must have been required to navigate sailing ships to the dockside, but by 1827 Portreath was described as Cornwall's most important port. It became known as Basset's Cove due to its association with the famous mining family who resided at nearby Tehidy, but *Porth Treth,* 'sandy cove', was first recorded as far back as 1485. A cholera outbreak in 1878 caused the death of almost half the population, and by 1886 the copper trade had collapsed and the port was nearly bankrupt, although trade of potatoes, coal, cement and slate continued until after WW2. Now only an occasional fishing boat operates from the harbour, while the village has been transformed into an attractive place to live or holiday. The harbour is part of the Cornish Mining World Heritage Site, although some of that heritage has been dissipated by the construction of some plain and unattractive houses. It hit the headlines when stormy weather in 2014 resulted in repairs estimated to have cost £500,000, while 2018 saw a 65ft section of the harbour wall destroyed with hundreds of tons of masonry crashing onto the sand below.

The beach lies to the west of the harbour wall, backed by imposing high cliffs and a convenient car park, big enough for 160 cars. It's predominantly sandy with patches of shingle, and there's a fair-sized beach even at high water, while low water sees it extend over 500yds to include Amy's Cove, also called Smugglers' Cove, and beyond towards Western Hill. Amy was the wife of a customs officer who lived in a cottage above the beach; his job was to prevent smuggling but, in true Cornish style, a secret tunnel led from behind a large fireplace in the cottage to a cave below! At low water the beach is around 240yds deep and there are a number of rock pools at both ends, notably in the rocky area beneath the harbour wall where there's also a natural bathing pool. On the western side are six smaller bath-shaped pools that were carved out of the rocks during the 19th century to enable Lady Frances Basset to enjoy the healing powers of seawater. A stream runs across the middle of the beach, dissipating beyond the high water mark; at the height of the mining industry the stream and sea were stained red with copper ore. Dog restrictions apply and the beach is cleaned daily throughout the summer. A powerful storm in January 2016 revealed the remains of a petrified forest, believed to be between 4,000 and 6,000 years old. It is thought that the forest was growing during the Neolithic period but it became submerged when sea levels rose around the Cornish coast. Scenes from the 1946 film *The Rake's Progress,* starring Rex Harrison, were filmed here.

RNLI Lifeguards patrol throughout the summer and it's advisable to swim only when they are present due to dangerous rip currents. It may also be possible with care on a rising high tide on a calm day when there is little swell. The *Portreath Life Saving Club* was formed in 1958 after a young boy was drowned the previous year and their impressive clubhouse can be seen by the main entrance to the beach. Portreath is popular with surfers and bodyboarders, who flock here at high water to surf a hollow and dangerous break, known as the Vortex, by the harbour wall. Only the experienced should attempt this wave, everyone else should keep to the middle of the beach; tuition is available from *HQ Surf School*. Safety equipment can be found at various points above the beach and in the harbour.

Steps provide easy access from the car park and road, while there's a slipway at Amy's Cove. There's a fair amount of roadside parking in the village, which can also boast what must be the most colourful public toilets in the UK! *The Atlantic Café* is situated by the car park, tempting visitors with alluring aromas of bacon or fish and chips, and there is a pub and other restaurants and shops elsewhere in the village.

50. NORTH CLIFFS' BEACHES
SW 641 446 – SW 595 428
P, PT, RP, DA

After leaving Portreath the coastline rises rapidly to form the intimidating North Cliffs, which provide an exhilarating walk to Godrevy Point, five miles away. With the exception of a couple of valleys at the Portreath end it's a surprisingly level walk, with spectacular views of the steep, often sheer cliffs that average over 200ft in height. At the foot of the cliffs are numerous small coves and inlets bearing names such as Deadman's Cove – there are two of them - and Hell's Mouth, underlining the fearsome reputation of the cliffs, which have been the site of a multitude of shipwrecks. It may seem an unlikely setting in which to find any beaches, but some of the coves are decorated with alluring golden sand and linked to the clifftop by steep, often tortuous paths.

That alone would make for difficult access but additional danger is posed by the crumbling nature of the cliffs, which are composed of sandstone and shale laid down some 370 million years ago. These rock materials are weathered and have variable strength, resulting in catastrophic landslides and heavy erosion; because of this, the access paths to the beaches are fraught with danger and venturing down should only be attempted with extreme caution, or not attempted at all.

Heading westwards from Portreath, the beaches are: Porthcadjack Cove (SW 641 446), Basset's Cove (SW 637 441), Greenbank Cove (SW 630 435), Deadman's Cove (SW 625 432), and Fishing Cove (SW

595 428). Of these, Fishing Cove (Photo 1) is the easiest to access, but even that requires great care and a head for heights as the path meanders around the back of the cove before descending steeply at the far end. Be aware that it can be very slippery in places when wet, but ropes have been provided to aid the final tricky descent (Photo 3). Despite these hazards the path is regularly used by those determined to visit what is a beautiful, north-facing beach of golden sand and turquoise sea. There is usually a strip of sand even at high water, at least in the summer. When the tide is out it's possible to walk around to the adjacent Castle Giver Cove, also known as Smuggler's Cove, a popular naturist beach, which may explain why the access path is so well trodden. The name comes from *Porth Castel Gaver*, 'cove of the goat's castle'. Because it is otherwise inaccessible, always make sure to be back at Fishing Cove before the tide returns. The surrounding cliffs provide shelter from westerly winds but also cause the beach to be in shadow for much of the day. It's not advisable to sit beneath the cliffs due to the danger of falling rocks. There are rock pools on both sides and dogs are allowed all year. Keep an eye out for seals, which frequently use these isolated coves for breeding. Swimming is possible with care on a calm day and a rising high tide, but definitely not at low water. There is good snorkelling in calm conditions during the summer. The narrowness of the cove and undersea rocks are not ideal for surfing but it is possible, with care, when conditions are favourable. There is no safety equipment. The nearest facilities are at Godrevy, where there is a café and toilets, and there's a seasonal café at Hell's Mouth. There's a car park big enough for 20 cars nearby, just off the B3301, and a larger car park at Hell's Mouth.

Of the other beaches, Basset's Cove (Photo 2), known as Spratting Cove until the 1880s, was a favourite of the Basset family, who built a summerhouse there. In 1896 a path was created to provide easy access but it has eroded over the years and now it's a steep and treacherous descent, the dangers highlighted by a dramatic cliff collapse that was caught on camera in 2011. Accessing Porthcadjack involves a hair-raising, rope assisted descent down an almost sheer scree slope, with the spray from an impressive waterfall adding to the adversity after heavy rain. A nearby cliff collapse in 2019 underlined the problems posed by erosion, making access to this and the other beaches exceptionally hazardous and suitable only for the very determined and very experienced cliff climber.

BIBLIOGRAPHY

ACTON, BOB: Around Newquay (1990)
ACTON, BOB: Around Perranporth, St Agnes and Portreath (2005)
BARING-GOULD, SABINE: In the Roar of the Sea (1892)
BARTON, R M (Ed): Life in Cornwall in the Early 19th Century (1970)
BARTON R M (Ed): Life in Cornwall in the Mid-19th Century (1971)
BARTON R M (Ed): Life in Cornwall in the Late 19th Century (1972)
BARTON R M (Ed): Life in Cornwall at the End of the 19th Century (1974)
BETJEMAN, JOHN, Betjeman's Cornwall (1988)
BETJEMAN, JOHN: Summoned By Bells (1960)
COLLINS, WILKIE: Rambles Beyond Railways (1861)
FOOT, SARAH: Rivers of Cornwall (1984)
GRAHAM, WINSTON: Poldark's Cornwall (1983)
HARPER, SHEILA: Newquay Through Time (2013)
HIND, C LEWIS: Days in Cornwall (1907)
INGREY, JACK: St Merryn: Its Bays and Byways (1983)
INGREY, JACK: St Minver: Its Bays and Byways (1994)
INGREY, JACK: The Camel Footpath (1984)
JOHN, CATHERINE R: The Saints of Cornwall (2001)
NANCE, DAMIAN & BROWN, KENNETH: The Engine Houses of West Cornwall (2014)
PADEL, O J: Cornish Place-Names (1988)
RAWE, DONALD R and INGREY, JACK: Padstow and District (1984)
SALMON, ARTHUR L: Cornwall (1910)
TREGARTHEN, ENYS: North Cornwall Fairies and Legends (1906)
TREGARTHEN, ENYS: The Piskey Purse (1905)